THE
FLOWER OF GLOSTER

THE
FLOWER OF GLOSTER

E. Temple Thurston

With an introduction and
commentary to illustrations by
David Viner

ALAN SUTTON
1987

Alan Sutton Publishing Limited
30 Brunswick Road
Gloucester GL1 1JJ

First published 1911
This illustrated edition published 1984
Reprinted 1987

Copyright © in this edition, Alan Sutton Publishing Limited 1984
Copyright © in introduction, David Viner 1984

British Library Cataloguing in Publication Data

   Thurston, E. Temple
      The Flower of Gloster.
      1. Inland navigation—England 2. England
      —Description and travel—1901–1945
      I. Title
      914.2′0483   DA630

   ISBN 0-86299-177-3 (case)
   ISBN 0-86299-305-9 (paper)

Photoset Bembo 11/13
Typesetting and origination
Alan Sutton Publishing Limited
Printed in Great Britain

INTRODUCTION

The Flower of Gloster was first published in 1911, and was sufficiently well received to encourage its publishers Williams & Norgate to produce a new edition two years later. Subsequently a cheap and unillustrated edition appeared (Chapman & Hall, 1918), followed by fifty years during which this account of a journey around the canals of the south midlands remained out of print.

It did not, however, disappear from view. When the canal historian and enthusiast Tom Rolt set down his own canal experiences nearly thirty years later in *Narrow Boat* (not published until 1944), he looked back to Temple Thurston's account with delight, recalling that it occupied pride of place in his own collection of canal literature. This collection was by no means extensive and Rolt was able to identify Temple Thurston as the only professional writer amongst those whose accounts and recollections of canal journeys had appeared in print in the previous half-century.

In his own foreword to *Narrow Boat,* H.J. Massingham – perhaps the doyen in the field of rural literature – identified Temple Thurston's 'pleasant volume' as a rare contribution to a neglected subject, a source of interest and fascination quite untapped by other writers. Thus when the first wave of the considerable output in publications on the history of British canals began to appear in the 1960s, it was not surprising to find L.T.C. Rolt contributing an introduction to a new edition of *The Flower of Gloster* (David & Charles 1968 and 1972).

This edition too in its turn has been out of print for some years and I well recall discovering copies of both *Narrow Boat* and *The Flower of Gloster* together on the shelves of a second-hand bookshop in Cirencester one Saturday morning ten years or so ago. What a happy chance that brought me to such a fund of nostalgia and enthusiasm!

Narrow Boat remains in print and to those who have come to know and love the British canal system and its history it remains a classic. Temple Thurston's volume deserves to stand alongside, for it too conjures up a vision of a vanished age, a way of life which existed within the framework of English society but which remained strangely – and firmly – aloof from it right through until the eventual demise of the community of people who lived and worked upon the canal system in England.

The Flower of Gloster is above all things a romance, a 'voyage of discovery' (p. 63), but cast in a very distinctive mould, related partially to the author's own approach to his work and partially to the subject of canals. To appreciate the full value of the account it is necessary to examine both aspects.

Ernest Temple Thurston was a prolific novelist and playwright who produced more than a title per year between 1905 and 1933. Born in 1879, he had two volumes of poems in print by the time he was seventeen and two years later had written (although not published) his first work Apple of Eden. His first four-act play Red and White Earth had been produced in the provinces in 1902 and thereafter from 1905-32 his output totalled forty novels (in twenty-eight years, missing only 1923 and 1931) plus two volumes of poems and eleven plays. Much of this seems today to have been assigned to oblivion and only The Flower of Gloster now survives in print. There are various reasons for this, some of which help us to understand Temple Thurston's own view of this work.

In 1901 Temple Thurston married Katherine Cecil Madden, herself a writer and producer of four novels during the ten years of their marriage. Temple Thurston was in fact married three times, his first two wives divorcing him in 1910 and 1924 respectively. His marriages thus lasted for nine, thirteen and eight years before his own death from pneumonia at the early age of 53 in March 1933. The Flower of Gloster appeared in 1911 and purports to describe a journey undertaken during May (of 1910 or 1911?). Two titles preceded it in 1910, The Garden of Resurrection also appeared in 1911 and another title the following year. Two plays also belong to this period, which seems to have been a particularly productive one in Temple Thurston's life.

The author's own dedication is dated August 1911 and tells us that he offers the volume as a wedding present to 'Bellwattle'. This must surely be Joan Katherine Cann, whom he married in that year at about the same time that his first wife died. Perhaps the personal turmoil which might be associated with this period is referred to in the dedication and Temple Thurston's desire to escape on his 'voyage of discovery' was sharpened by events in his own personal life?

Certainly a journey by canal would offer escapism in a very distinct form, and there is ample evidence that Temple Thurston both fully welcomed and appreciated this experience. He found the canal into Stratford-on-Avon 'right out of the track of the world' (p. 71) and much of the book's strength comes from his ability to capture the isolation and steady pace of canal life.

Massingham noted that the English canal system was less well-known than the Solomon Islands and that the decline in commercial use of the waterways had removed those who lived and worked on them from the public eye into a sort of transport limbo. Today, with extensive leisure use of canals and a continually expanding popular literature about them, it is

difficult to appreciate the obscurity of the world into which Temple
Thurston ventured and which both he and Tom Rolt in later years captured
in print. Indeed the canals themselves had their own distinctive characteristic
each from the other, and the route of *The Flower of Gloster* included at least
three of the most attractive and individualistic canals in the southern
midlands. So too the individuals who populated them. The southern Oxford
Canal boasted right through to the end of its commercial working life the
individual boat owners – or 'Number Ones' – who so attracted Rolt and later
writers. Although it is doubtful if Temple Thurston's own boatman
Eynsham Harry was a 'number one' in the true sense, he certainly rings true
as a character in this mould and remains one of the lasting memories from
the whole account.

On the face of it Temple Thurston's journey followed a logical and
circular route. Having made contact and secured an arrangement in Oxford,
he then followed the Oxford Canal northwards on its circuitous route to join
the great network of the midland canal system roughly where Oxfordshire,
Northamptonshire and Warwickshire meet north of Banbury. From here he
followed through Warwick and Leamington on the line into Birmingham,
an experience which grew less and less palatable. Retracing his route back
thence into the countryside, Temple Thurston opted for the southern
Stratford Canal into that town, this section giving him great scope for
philosophising on the condition of man in general. Indeed both the Oxford
and Stratford sections are strong on the author's contemplations – a diet
which perhaps we find too sweet and untempered for today's taste.
Certainly this is no dry travelogue, and the combination of delightful
description with a strong flavour of Edwardian romanticism is one of the
major attractions of *The Flower of Gloster*.

From Stratford the canal system was temporarily abandoned in favour of a
cross-country walk following the banks of the Warwickshire Avon to
Evesham and Tewkesbury where both author, boatman and narrow boat
rejoined. But then follows a mystery: the logical next stage in the circular
route was from Tewkesbury down the river Severn (always an interesting
experience) to Gloucester docks, and thence by canal to Stroud. None of this
appears at all, and for years I harboured the hope that a missing chapter from
Temple Thurston's account might be hidden away somewhere. Finally, the
journey back to Oxford is via the Thames & Severn Canal from Stroud to
Lechlade, a route much loved but now – alas, said Rolt – abandoned and
derelict.

Thus the simple journey in a large circuit from Oxford via Banbury,
Warwick, Stratford, Evesham, Tewkesbury and Stroud to Oxford again is
not such a simple account as it may appear. The reader is, I think, asked now
to look at *The Flower of Gloster* at more than one level. Firstly, as the work of
a prolific novelist, it should be read as part of an extensive fictional output
and indeed as a significant contribution to the work of a writer strong on

sentimentality. This latter was marked enough for the Times obituary (20 March 1933) to note coyly that 'there were those who might suggest that sentimentalism was too evident in Temple Thurston's work . . .' At this level, the volume was and remains a good story, capturing lost images and introducing rural as well as canal themes for consideration. Had it remained no more than that, undoubtedly *The Flower of Gloster* would have disappeared into obscurity with much – if not all – of the remainder of Temple Thurston's work.

But it has not. Why? Without doubt Rolt's comments in 1944 (and reinforced again in 1968) were a major influence. He did not question its authenticity and subsequent canal historians and topographers have followed in similar vein, in print at least. So it has become a minor classic of a canal literature which is particularly concerned with nostalgia, so great have been the changes on the canals of England since the volume was written. As a contribution to a retrospective archive it is invaluable, hence the integration into the present edition of Temple Thurston's text not only of some of his own photographs but also other contemporary canal and rural scenes.

For the accuracy of the canal record, however, it is necessary to probe a little deeper and examine the account for its veracity. Is it, after all, merely a fictional account? Did the journey ever take place in its entirety or are we reading an account worked up from a series of individual – and separate – observations and experiences of canals and canal life in the first decade of this century? Is the value and interest of *The Flower of Gloster* thus diminished in any way?

I was first drawn to Temple Thurston's account – as I suspect were many other readers – by that part of his journey which followed the Thames & Severn Canal through the Cotswolds. This includes a description of Sapperton tunnel and the sheer exhaustion of 'legging' the boat through. This part of the account I knew first and still know best, and here some doubts of accuracy began to appear. With the opportunity to examine the entire account afresh and study much of the route on the ground today, my first reservations were reinforced, with the conclusion that I now feel *The Flower of Gloster* to be a clever interweaving of a series of different experiences, some of which have overlapped causing errors of detail in the reworking. Even so, *The Flower of Gloster* has lost none of its appeal, and remains today a fascinating record.

When the author struck his bargain to hire a narrow boat he wanted a journey of a month and this was the agreed period of hire. The first few days northwards from Oxford are well-documented and the timing makes sense. The first night was spent at Shipton-on-Cherwell (p. 27). seven miles north of the city, after a late afternoon start. Thereafter there are references to overnight stays at Banbury (p. 36), Warwick (p. 62) and later on at Little Cumberton (p. 104) beyond Evesham. The promise of a regular timetable suggested in the early sections travelling north from Oxford is not sustained and by the time the author and his boatman have met up again at Tewkesbury only three more days remained of their month's agreement (p. 106). Not even the most optimistic of boatmen would face the river journey to Gloucester plus the long journey along three canals (Gloucester & Berkeley, Stroudwater and Thames & Severn) with equanimity.

Add to this Temple Thurston's own decision-making at Stratford (p. 88) and the evidence seems to suggest a poor understanding of the total journey seen as a *complete* unit as distinct from a series of disparate experiences. Having made a firm decision against progress further into the Black Country (citizens of Solihull might not agree with this association!), Temple Thurston allows Eynsham Harry only one day from Stratford to rejoin him at Evesham, further down the river Avon. As the river was not navigable to *The Flower of Gloster*, the boatman was thus obliged to take an extensive detour on the canal system, into Birmingham on the northern Stratford to King's Norton and then down the heavily-locked 24 miles of the Worcester & Birmingham Canal, completing the journey by the river Severn to Tewkesbury and the Avon up to Evesham. It was not an agreement which suggests much knowledge of the canal and river network outside Temple Thurston's own route! As it was, the author eventually walked into Tewksbury before the pair met up again. It seems something of an understatement to regard this aspect of the journey as a little miscalculation.

On the Oxford and again on the southern Stratford, Temple Thurston's account has much which even today the interested observer would recognise and appreciate; the author captures the remoteness of both routes, aptly describing his travels 'through these countless places, hidden in the nooks and crannies of England'. Some of the vignettes are themselves enchanting episodes; who cannot call to mind the Red Lion at Cropredy on the Oxford north of Banbury and the two farm-workers refreshing their thirst (p. 48)? Equally the old man on the canal bridge at Lowson Ford on the Stratford in chapter XXVII.

As to characters, Eynsham Harry himself is well worthy of study. A boatman from the Coventry area – he gives his address as the lock cottage at Hillmorton on the northern Oxford Canal – he was doubtless drawn from real life, and the strength of his character (and indeed importance in the story as a whole) lends support to the view that Temple Thurston spent some time and did whatever 'research' he was able to do largely on the Oxford Canal. This route from the Warwickshire coalfield down to Oxford via Braunston and Napton junctions was long the preserve of 'number ones' who owned and operated their own working boats. Horse-drawn working boats bringing coal along this route continued right up until 1959 when Joe and Rose Skinner finally retired with their horse narrow boat *Friendship*.

If Temple Thurston walked along lengths of the Oxford and 'bridge-hopped' by hitching boat rides with the 'number ones' he would certainly have gathered a body of material well capable of being rounded in his fertile brain into Eynsham Harry. But did the man himself ever exist? Others have asked this question before and there is a view that Eynsham Harry might have been modelled on Harry Humphries, a boatman who came from Eynsham and who died some thirty years ago. It was commonplace for boatmen to be named after their place of origin and Eynsham, on the river Thames just west of Oxford, undoubtedly did produce men experienced in working on the river and into the canal system.

Strange therefore to find Eynsham Harry living up at Hillmorton, although this may simply reflect the new status of *The Flower of Gloster,* in the ownership of a Coventry boat-owner Joseph Phipkin and recently 'done up' at Braunston. Previously she had worked on the Thames & Severn Canal, and by implication the river Thames, and so the river may well have been familiar territory for both Eynsham Harry and *The Flower of Gloster.* Or perhaps it was Phipkin who was based at Hillmorton? Certainly *he* did exist and appears in a splendid photograph together with two of his horse boats at Buckby Locks on the Grand Union Canal (p. 17) a few years before Temple Thurston's own journey. Should the records survive it would be possible to trace the history of *The Flower of Gloster* and something of its working life, but what a mammoth task! In any case, is the name of the boat a piece of fiction too? It does ring true in canal parlance, and the association with the Thames & Severn in Gloucestershire adds credence; is there any other evidence of this name in actual use on the canals?

Harry Humphries had a brother, also a boatman and known as Eynsham Sam and it is interesting that one of the boatmen's names which occurs in Temple Thurston's text is Sam (p. 32) – another slight clue perhaps? So to the *Henrietta,* Eynsham Harry's own boat, which he offered to Temple Thurston for a future excursion . . . a typical narrow boat name from the midland canals.

For the observant canal historian, there are a number of irregularities in the text which come to notice. They may well add support to the idea of a piecemeal composition. One of the most glaring is the use of the word 'barge' throughout instead of the correct term of 'boat'. Barges were used on rivers and wider canals, leaving the ubiquitous boat for the system of narrow canals, based upon a seven-foot width, of which the Oxford Canal was and remains a classic example. No self-respecting boatman on this canal at least would have had anything to do with a barge! Similarly some of the specific references to canal activity are a little off the mark too, suggesting that overlapping of recollections has taken place. Three together (p. 32) just north of Oxford raise doubts – the reference to a Shropshire Union boat with a cargo of gas-water (for the production of ammonia) and a Fellows Morton boat carrying straw both seem strange loads for such companies, as is the reference to a 'fly boat out of Birmingham' i.e. a fast passenger boat, which would have been a rarity indeed on the Oxford Canal at that time.

One of Eynsham Harry's anecdotes of interest concerns the effect of setting fire to a bush – thus incinerating a thrush sitting on her nest – and caused from the spark of a steamer, one of the prestige boats which were in use on canals before the widespread adoption of the diesel engine. Such steamers indeed operated on the Grand Union but it is difficult to find evidence of them working fly-boats on the Oxford Canal. So perhaps both recollections came from elsewhere on the canal system, and maybe nearer London?

It could be argued that Temple Thurston did not travel for any significant distance at all on his *Flower of Gloster*. Certainly it would have been perfectly possible to study his selected or adopted route entirely by train, travelling out to one point on the canal system, walking some length of towpath and returning by train to his destination. Thus apart from Oxford and Banbury as the main railway stations along the Oxford Canal line, he could have gained access at Aynho (where the trains still disturb the peace of the canal alongside) and at Fenny Compton amongst others. As to Warwick, Leamington and the network of lines which would have taken him into Stratford-on-Avon, there would have been little difficulty in gaining access to the canal-side at numerous points. Is it significant that the whole of the area around Napton is described without apparent interest and what would have been a memorable journey through the locks around Warwick – particularly the flight at Hatton – remains indistinct in the account? Knowle flight of six locks (now five) is mentioned but by then the lockage worked by Eynsham Harry would have been considerable. Or is Knowle (p. 68) a symbol of them all?

It would thus seem logical to regard Temple Thurston's riverside walk from Stratford to Tewkesbury as coming from another part of his experience, and to see the entire journey from Oxford to Stratford as an accumulation of observations, undertaken with not a little assistance from the Great Western Railway. The otherwise inexplicable absence of the section from Tewkesbury through Gloucester to Stroud thus makes sense only because it was conveniently omitted.

When one comes finally to examine the Thames & Severn part of the account, the bias both of Temple Thurston and indeed of Rolt needs to be stated. In his ruminatings (p. 111) during the journey Temple Thurston declared a particular fondness for the Thames & Severn . . . 'such beauties as I shall ever remember' . . . and he did spend some of his later life in Gloucestershire. Rolt too felt deeply the loss of the Thames & Severn to navigation and some part of his working life too had been spent in the county. Small wonder that the photographs selected for the 1968 edition from Temple Thurston's own album taken at the time of his account show a distinct bias towards this section of the journey. Five of the eight prints used in 1968 depict the Stonehouse–Lechlade section, and in the original edition three of W.R. Dakin's six colour plates.

A systematic study of the Thames & Severn material from Temple

Thurston's album suggests that none of the photographs need have been taken far from one of the railway stations at various points along the canal line.

The details of photographs and their relationship to the text is examined in the commentary to the illustrations.

A final query comes very much at the end of the account. If Eynsham Harry was as familiar with the Thames & Severn and the river Thames as we might suggest, why did he turn in the pound at Inglesham at the very entrance into the river Thames and proceed to return all the way retracing his journey to get back to Coventry and Mr. Phipkin? The quicker route – and arguably one easier to work too – would have taken him down the river directly to Oxford and then into the Oxford Canal again. Did Temple Thurston confuse his west to east account along the Thames & Severn with an east to west recollection of his own travels? This might explain some minor inconsistencies plus the more obvious error of confusing the emergence of *The Flower of Gloster* from Sapperton tunnel into the setting sun with a boat rising up to meet them in the next lock. These experiences no doubt left a clear impression, but *The Flower of Gloster* would have been travelling westwards, and not eastwards from the tunnel.

But enough. Specific doubts such as these are all very well and may serve to balance the record until some firmer evidence appears (do Temple Thurston's manuscripts survive, I wonder?). They should not, however, draw too much attention away from the main value of the account and probably one of the author's main aims in producing *The Flower of Gloster* . . . the telling of a very good story from strong visual images observed 'on the cut' and at a time in the author's life when he was perhaps particularly susceptible to the need to escape from reality into a hidden and fascinating world.

Some part of the route followed by *The Flower of Gloster* can still be followed by canal today; other sections have gone from view. A note on these is included with the commentary to the illustrations.

For the first edition, none of Temple Thurston's own photographs were used; instead – and true to the conventions of the day – they were used as reference material by the artist W.R. Dakin whose sketches illuminate not only the 1911 and 1913 editions but the 1968 edition too. His six colour plates were probably also worked up from the photographs. Indeed Dakin's illustrations were used for visual effect throughout the volume and not necessarily in a correct relationship between the provenance of the original photograph and the text. Where original photographs have been re-used here, an effort has been made to provenance them correctly.

Corrections or errors, further information and any additional evidence on this fascinating account of a canal journey would be welcomed from readers.

David Viner   July 1984

London,
August 1911.

My dear Bellwattle,

A wedding present is always inadequate. I have no doubt if I gave you a dog, you would be best pleased with that; but you have Dandy, and lavish such affection on him as makes me at times regard him in the light of a thief; I have thought of other things besides dogs, and am reduced at last to offering you this — this chronicle of the journey of the *Flower of Gloster*. If ever it takes you — only for one hour — away from the need of forgetfulness to the joy of remembrance, then in some sense this little wedding present will not be so inadequate as it may seem.

Your Cruikshank.

P.S. — Thirteen copies count as twelve. This will well-nigh lead you into the higher mathematics when you come to calculate your royalties.

PUBLISHED WORKS OF
ERNEST TEMPLE THURSTON (1879–1933)

1895	(two volumes of poems)	1919	The Forest Fire
1902	Red and White Earth (play)		Sheepskins and Grey Russet
1905	The Apple of Eden	1920	The World of Wonderful Reality
1906	Traffic		The Wandering Jew (play)
1907	The Evolution of Katherine	1921	The Green Bough
	The Realist	1922	The Eye of the Wift
1908	Sally Bishop		The Miracle
	Mirage	1923	A Roof and Four Walls (play)
1909	The City of Beautiful Nonsense		Judas Iscariot (play)
1910	The Greatest Wish in the World		Poems 1918-23
	The Patchwork Papers	1924	May Eve
1911	The Garden of Resurrection		Charmeuse
	The Flower of Gloster		The Blue Peter (play)
	Sally Bishop (play)	1925	Mr. Bottleby Does Something
1912	The Antagonists	1926	The Rosetti
	The Greatest Wish (play)		The Goose Feather Bed
1913	The Open Window,	1927	Jane Carroll
	and Richard Furlong		Come and Listen
1914	The Achievement	1928	Portrait of a Spy
	Driven (play)	1929	The King's Candle
	The Cost (play)		Millenium
1915	Tares		Emma Hamilton (play)
	The Passionate Crime	1930	The Rosicrucian
1916	The Five-Barred Gate		Man in a Black Hat
1917	Enchantment		Charmeuse (play)
	Over the Hill	1932	A Hank of Hair
	Summer (poems)		Broken Heart
1918	David & Jonathan	1933	Son of Man (play)

see also Digressions ed. 'Bellwattle', being extracts from the works of E. Temple Thurston (nd).

THE

'FLOWER OF GLOSTER'

I

THE DISCOVERER

I have ever believed that the world is a place to wander in. Indeed, if Time be made for slaves, then Space is made for freemen. It is only the freeman who, one bright morning, when the long brown buds like cornucopias are bursting on the beech tree, can sling a knapsack across his shoulders, drop the key of the house in the deepest corner of his pocket, and set out down the road of discovery.

An open door, they say, will tempt a saint. If the temptation be to wander forth into a wide and wonderful world where every man, if he have but the heart for it, may be his own discoverer, then I can well believe the truth of all they say. Now, of open doors there may be many, and of saints who yield to their temptation, no less. But the heart for the spirit of discovery, that is a different business altogether. You will as like find it in a sinner as a saint. There are few, indeed who have it now.

For this, I would urge you, is the spirit of discovery; not merely that setting of one's prow towards the far horizon of the unknown – that is the spirit of adventure. The spirit of discovery lies in the eye and in the mind. He whose sight is young enough to find anew the world that has been found by others, he is the discoverer and, by right of that power of which he holds the secret, a man may reveal new worlds wherever he goes.

There is none too much of that spirit left in any of us now. Guide-books and the like have taken all the freshness out of our point of view. A man travels to see what others have seen before him; he buys his beauties of the road at second hand. They go so far as to give him reduction for a quantity. Cheap tours comprising the greatest number of sights in the shortest space of time are innovations our Grandfathers would have shuddered at. They read books of travel in those days. But your guide is no traveller. He knows his beauties off by heart as the verger knows the little history of his church. So well does he know them, moreover, that they are no longer beauties for him, but only catch-words set to trap the tourist's ear.

'This Tower,' says he, with a ready eye to mark his listener's face, 'was built in the year of our Lord——' And when he says 'the year of our Lord,' he means to astonish you then.

I remember the showman in the Whispering Gallery of St. Paul's. As I entered by the narrow doorway into that vast space beneath the dome, a tiny little man in a black gown took me in hand at once, at once began pouring forth his monotonous doggerel of facts – figures of height and breadth and depth. The Lord himself knows what they were, for I have long forgotten them.

'Now go,' said he, 'round to the other side, and I'll whisper to you.'

In the hands of such men as these, somehow or other, one is numbed into obedience. Meekly I went. Then, as he leant his head against the wall, there came from the lips of this insignificant little creature a voice which, in one great volume of sound, shook me and made me tremble as it thundered by.

'Can you hear what I'm saying?' shouted the voice.

When I replied that I could, he nodded his head to me across the mighty gulf and smiled as one who well approves of himself. Had he been Sir Christopher himself, he could not have looked more pleased.

For a few moments, then, I sat there opposite the door looking down alone into the chasm of the nave. But only for a few moments was I allowed to marvel at the wonder of it all; only for a few moments was I allowed to discover it for myself. At the very commencement of my meditations, there entered two more visitors through the door, and the little man began again his miserable rigmarole of heights and breadths and depths.

I bethought me then of an excellent thing to do, and, leaning my head against the wall, I whispered in the sweetest voice I knew:

'For God's sake stop that silly nonsense!'

For the brief space of time in which my voice must take to travel round, I looked across and waited. A second later I saw him stagger, and the visitors, frightened, looked about them as the thunder of my words resounded in their ears.

A whispering gallery, you may perceive, has its advantages; but a guide, so far as I have ever been able to discover, has none. He would willingly ruin every illusion you might have.

'Around that corner,' says he, 'you will come face to face with St. Mark's and the four bronze horses——'

But for Heaven's sake, say I, let me turn the corner for myself. What else was a corner made for but to hide at once the beauties it reveals!

Yet that is never the spirit of the guide, for the guide-book is his litany.

'I'll go,' said I one day, 'where are no guides and scarce a map is printed. Who knows his way about the canals of England?'

'They begin at Regent's Park,' said a man.

'And then?' I asked him.

'There's one passes near Slough on the Great Western. I've seen it from the train.'

'If that's all that's known about them,' said I, 'I'll get a barge myself and go on till I stop.'

II

THE 'FLOWER OF GLOSTER'

These things are easily said. It is the devil and all to accomplish them. Everyone I knew, I asked, 'Where can I get a barge?'

It was a foolish question to make, and one to which, as often as not, I received the foolish reply, 'What for?'

What in the name of Heaven could one want a barge for, unless it were in which to travel on those waters where all barges may be found? Out of its element, doubtless, it is the ugliest thing the hand of man ever created; but sinking low in the still waters of those silent canals, its blunt, good-natured nose thrusting the long ripples to either side, travelling from one old town to another with its happy-go-lucky two and three miles an hour, it is the most wonderful vehicle in the world.

There came a time when I grew sick of that answer. Then I went down to the Regent's Park Basin, where all those barges going east, west, and north, collect and discharge their cargo.

'Hire a barge?' said they. 'Where do you want to go?'

'Anywhere,' I replied. 'You don't think I'm looking for an express method of conveyance.'

They gazed from one to the other with amusement that was more or less respectful. The world is full of fools, of course, and none so great a fool is there as he who would think to find time for play with that which is another man's labour. They did not say as much as this. They thought it in their several ways, every single one of them. I doubt if I should have known as much respect to the man who came and asked me where he could get pens, ink, and paper, for that he was going to spend his holidays a-writing.

But the bargee, notwithstanding all that reputation he has earned, has the innate sense of politeness which only the breeding of nature can give to a man. More than half his days, gliding peacefully through those winding stretches of water, with the great breadth of a glorious country on either side of him, he is in closest touch with the best that nature has to give. Often without education, without even the knowledge of how to read or write, he lives a life of complete and untouched simplicity. He is a law almost to himself.

Now they would have you believe, the apostles of civilisation, that man is a social creature, thriving, developing, progressing through the medium of the community. That elusive word – gentleman – which no one understands and few can emulate, has been coined by a class calling itself Society. Society has bred the gentleman, just as the Irish have bred the race-horse, the only difference being that the Irishman knows a race-horse when he sees it.

But just as the race-horse is not the only animal of that species in existence, so the gentleman is not the only man. What is more, he is not the only gentleman. The fact of the matter is, Society has lost its cunning in breeding the race. They have outbred the stock which made them famous. Nature can breed far finer gentlemen now than ever Society puts forth into the field. For it is not luxury which is the food for the species, but that work and that labour bringing the sweat honestly to the brow. And the bargee, for all his rough-and-readiness, is one of the many gentlemen of Nature I have met.

When, failing to discover at the Regent's Park Basin where I might hire a barge, I betook myself to headquarters and made inquiries at the offices of one of the canal navigations, I was told that I probably did not realise the class of men with whom I should have to mix.

'They're not gentlemen, you know,' said the officer with a smile. 'And if you take out a barge yourself, you'll probably come a great deal in contact with them.'

'Now what,' said I, 'do you mean by a gentleman?'

I think his smile was compassionate. For the moment he believed I was as ignorant of the matter as himself. Whereupon he shrugged his shoulders as one who would say: 'My dear sir – a gentleman? To a gentleman the term explains itself.'

But it was his shrug of the shoulders that I answered. What is more, I took the opportunity of translating it as I chose.

'You see,' said I, 'how unhappy a word that is. A shrug of the shoulders won't dispose of it. Nevertheless, in your opinion it comes to this – the bargee is not a gentleman. But if neither you nor I know what a gentleman is – for I swear to God that I don't, – why should it concern you that I hire a barge, or me that I must mix with bargees in the hiring of it?'

Now the offices of the canal navigation are dusty rooms. The dust hangs heavily on all the maps that surround the walls. Were it the office of a mortuary or the room of the little man who kept the records in the Morgue, there would be more business done there in an idle day. As it is, so far as I could see, the only company the officer keeps are his papers. To be suddenly confronted, then, by a strange individual, who immediately plunges into some abstruse controversy as to the meaning of the word gentleman, was a little more than he could bear. I think some of the dust of the office must long have got into his brain, for the more I said, the more confused he grew. Had I brought a feather brush with me and ruthlessly swept the dust from every shelf and cranny in the place, I could scarce have upset him more.

When, then, I saw him growing red in the face, I changed the subject.

'In any case,' said I, 'it concerns me more to know if I can hire a barge.'

'You can hire twenty,' he replied. 'But I prefer you did it than I. Do you intend to sleep on board?'

I confessed it had been my intention.

'Then you won't want an old manure barge?'

'I might feel a prejudice against that,' said I.

He fell to looking over some papers. Presently he raised his head.

'There's a barge at Oxford,' he informed me. 'She used to be on the Thames and Severn Canal – carried stone – wood sometimes. She's just been done up at Braunston and brought along there. If you went down there at once and saw the owner, he might hire her to you for a couple of months, and make a bit out of it himself.'

'What's her name?' said I.

'The *Flower of Gloster*.'

Now when he said that, then I knew she was mine. The *Flower of Gloster*! The name alone would have disinfected her of all the disagreeable odours in the world.

III

THE 'FLOWER OF GLOSTER'

continued

In matters of this kind, a fine sounding name has much to do with the success of the venture. Alice Louise may have been at heart a noble creature, meaning all that was admirable in a wife to the man who named his barge after her. But to you who know nothing of Alice Louise and all her sterling qualities, there is not that sweetness in the name which will destroy a cargo of gas-water of all its unpleasant odours.

If the clothes he wears, and the title he has won, have anything to do with your respect of a man, then look to the painting and the naming of your barge. And if she have half so fine a name as the *Flower of Gloster,* take her at once as I did. A coat of paint is, any day, an easier matter than a christening.

For Fate orders these things much to her own liking. All the ships that ever made history for England were nobly called. The *Bellerophon*! There was a boastful name, well chosen to carry into banishment the greatest maker of history the world has ever seen. Fate looked to it, too, that he was greatly named as well. What but great things could come to pass on the *Victory*? Where better could they happen than at Trafalgar!

With such a name as Nelson, battles at sea were made to be won; though, indeed, I knew a bank clerk of that surname who never so much as won the approbation of his manager. True, they had not christened him Horatio, and doubtless that made much of the difference.

'But all this,' said I, as the officer regarded my sudden decision with amazement, 'all this is a matter of sentiment and comes nowhere in our reckoning.'

''Twould be more to the point,' replied he, 'if you inquire the cost of the hiring.'

'At any price,' said I, 'the *Flower of Gloster* would be cheap.'

Whereupon he settled back in his chair, together with the dust that I had raised upon my entrance, and, thanking him, as any man should be thanked for coming so far out of his groove as to speak to me, I left him and set off for Oxford.

IV

OXFORD

'Down in the town, off the bridges and the grass
They are sweeping up the leaves to let the people pass,
Sweeping up the old leaves, golden-reds and browns,
Whilst the men go to lecture with the wind in their gowns.'

Frances Cornford wrote that of Cambridge – of an autumn morning, too. It kept singing in my head, nevertheless, as I walked through Oxford that morning in May to find my *Flower of Gloster*.

If a stanza be true in autumn, it is true in all the seasons beside. It mattered little whether it were Oxford or Cambridge to me. That the leaves were young and golden, just topping the old walls of the college gardens, giving you pictures framed preciously through the narrow doorways of the college gates; that it would be whole months of spring and summer before they fell again and raced with the gusty winds of autumn down the streets, made no difference to the simple truth of that little rhyme. The men *were* going to lecture, and the wind *was* in their gowns. So I lilted the lines to myself as I found my way down to the canal side.

'I ran out to the apple tree and plucked an apple down,
And all the bells were ringing in the old grey Town.'

''Tis the old grey Town that matters,' said I. 'We shall have the apples
fast enough.'

I don't care how dull or dusty may be the minds of the dons and
pedagogues who live within the walls of Oxford now. It is the old grey
Town that matters and the few customs that remain.

One New Year's eve I was taken to the college of Magdalen to hear the
carols sung. In a great hall with massive ceiling and with panelled walls
we were given mulled claret to drink, from Elizabethan silver jugs; plates
of mince-pies were handed round; all the old customs were observed to
the last letter. At some short time before midnight every illumination
was extinguished. Then by the light of a great fire burning brightly in the
open grate, with the reflection of its flames dancing on the polished oak,
winking from the silver jugs upon the long refectory tables, the choir
began its singing of the old-time English carols. But it is not that which I
remember best of all. As the hour of midnight struck and the New Year
was on the very threshold of the world, they flung wide open the great
windows and, through the old grey Town, we heard the pealing of a
hundred bells. It was as if each one of them with ringing voice were
crying out, "The Old Year is dead – long live the New!"

But for their buildings and their customs, all Oxford might be dead.
Even now it is a city of dust and shadows. The masters of learning who
sit in the deep-welled seats of their college windows, gazing across the
grave, green gardens, are no more than the myriad particles of decay
which slowly have been settling there upon the mullions for the last few
hundred years.

'When a man has had no Alma Mater other than the light of day and
such odd jests of chance as circumstance has chosen to shield him with,
then,' thought I, 'this is just the sort of thing he will be bound to say of the
universities.'

It is of more concern to everyone that I found my barge. But before
that be come to, I must say some word of the offices of the Oxford and
Birmingham Canal Navigation. How long they have been employed to
that purpose, I do not know. In comparison with the age of the building
it cannot have been for many years. It is built of that grey stone from
which all the colleges have been erected, and, by now, the yellow growth
of age has toned it to wonderful shades which bring colour both to your
imagination and your eye.

By a narrow wooden door in a high stone wall you are given sudden
entrance to a garden bright with colour, warm with the scent of flowers.
There, in spring, the violet aubrietia blends its masses with the faint blue
of the periwinkle; the double arabis spreads its carpet of snow before the
purple iris and the scarlet tulip buds.

In the midst of those drab surroundings where lies the canal quite close
to the railway station, this unexpected oasis of colour, hidden beyond

high walls which keep it from the eyes of the passers-by, is like a jewel set in lead. It was by chance I visited it – the same chance which has ever been my Alma Mater.

And on to this garden look the high windows of the canal company's offices. When I came there a shower of rain had just been falling and a thousand glittering diamond drops of water were hanging from the points of the leaves on the lilac trees. The air was cool, and the whole place was fresh with the light of a bright blue sky of spring.

'Were I the canal company's officer in Oxford,' said I to the manager in charge, 'this should be my pension.'

'I call it part of my salary, myself,' said he. 'Come out and see a new sort of sweet-scented stock I've got. One plant will scent a whole room.'

We went out to a little glass-house where he forces his young shoots and keeps the prize specimens of his horticulture. A tortoise was in somnolent charge of the whole establishment. If Bellwattle were here, thought I, how she would surprise the canal company's officer with an address to the tortoise! There was an animal who would have looked after her interests and God's as well without so much as making a fuss over the serving of two masters!

With an animated expression in his face, he expatiated to me upon one plant after another. I forget what he called this; I forget what he called that. They were all beautiful and they all had Latin names. When chance is your Alma Mater, you must pretend a knowledge of the dead languages and get along through this life as best you can.

'Indeed!' said I – and 'Yes!' said I to every name he gave.

Ignorance is a luxury only to be afforded by the very, very wise.

Could I but quote Latin, doubtless there would be much respect for me. But that I don't, probably loses me no more. There are always those who do not understand, and to put a man at that disadvantage when you have him in conversation is a risking of all his approval.

I only thought well of my canal official's knowledge because I contrived to deceive him that I knew as much myself. Had I known that he was aware of my ignorance, I should have disliked him very much indeed.

'What's your busiest time of the year here?' I asked him, when he had filled my head with names.

'Spring,' he replied.

I looked at the rows of boxes with their young shoots neatly thinned.

'I suppose it must be,' said I.

V

OXFORD – *continued*

But they know such a deuce of a lot in Oxford. They are too clever for me by half.

Into a curio shop, calling itself Lares & Penates, I walked – as is my weakness wherever a curio shop is to be found, – and there bought some little thing that had the taste of age about it. It was not that antiquity of which they make a special study in Birmingham, despatching to the old houses in the old towns of England where they will tell you it has been in the family for generations. Its age, at least, was genuine. Not that I know – but I say so.

'Send it round,' said I, 'to the inn where I am staying. I'll pay on delivery.'

And round it came in the care of a young man of twenty, who deposited it on my table and smiled. It was a warm day and, taking out his handkerchief, he wiped the perspiration from his brow.

'That will be another sixpence,' said I to myself. It was as plain as writing it on the bill.

'And to whom do I make out the cheque?' I asked.

'Lairs and Penaits,' said he.

I looked up with my pen raised.

'Lairs and Penaits,' he repeated.

'Will they understand that at the bank?' I inquired. For, mind you, I had not then seen their name above the door.

'Oh yes – Lairs and Penaits – they'll understand it all right. It means 'ousehold gods.'

Then I remembered. Latin syntax! It made me feel quite young again.

> 'Common are to either sex,
> Artifex and opifex.'

A doggerel rhyme of words which play some nasty tricks with your Latin exercise whenever you are fool enough to use them.

'You must forgive my asking,' said I.

'Oh well – it ain't everybody as knows,' he replied. 'Not even in Oxford. It's only when you're heducated, of course.'

I took my place without a word.

'I don't say that meaning nothin',' he continued. Perhaps he saw the look of humility on my face, and was thinking of his sixpence. No man will pay for the virtue of humility. It is not cheap at any price. Certainly it is not so cheap as it feels. Wherefore, hastening to reassure me, he added: 'I only came across it myself by chanst.'

'How's that?' said I.

'Well,' he replied, 'when I'm not doing messages for them, I do a bit of window-cleanin'. I saw it in a book. I was cleanin' the windows of a school. It was lyin' on a desk. Now I'm always sharp on them things. I'd sooner read a book like that than any novel. Lairs and Penaits – I saw it there in the book.'

'But which means household gods?' said I – 'Lairs or Penaits?'

'Well, both of them. Only, one's old Roman Latin, and the other's Italian Latin.'

I looked at him with envy.

'I wish I was educated like you,' said I.

'Well, you can't 'elp it 'ere in Oxford,' said he. 'I say it's the air of the place – it makes you want to know things like that.'

'And such a help to window-cleaning,' said I.

He glanced at me quickly.

'Ye–es,' said he – but oh! so very slowly! It might have been a word of two syllables.

VI

JOSEPH PHIPKIN – OWNER

Down by the canal wharf, I found the *Flower of Gloster*. What with her new paint, the thought too, no doubt, that soon she would be mine, I could have picked her out from a thousand others. Their ideas of colour are very southern, these people of the barges. Much is to be found of the gypsy in their habits, their appearance, and their minds. Indeed, they are no less than water gypsies, having that same barbaric, Latin eye for colour with the painting of their boats as the country gypsy has for the decoration of his caravan.

The exterior of the cabin in the aft part of the boat is gaily painted with vivid reds, glaring yellows, greens, and black. Water-cans, buckets, the shallow pails for the horse's provender, even the horse's traces too – a set of wooden beads strung loose upon a cord – all are painted with their Spanish joy of colour. And this is not the closest relation of their minds to that country which has fed the world with gypsies. I puzzled for a long while before I realised that the scenes which are painted on the panels on their cabin exteriors are rough pictures of those castles, not which you build, but which you find in Spain. What is more, these people are lovers of brass – a sure sign of the gypsy. Inside many a cabin of the boats which ply their long journeys and are the only homes of those who work them, you will find the old brass candlesticks, brass pots and pans, all brilliantly polished, glittering in the light. A brass lamp hangs from the bulkhead. It does not swing, for the motion of these barges is like to no other vehicle

in which I have ever ridden. It is no motion, or it is motion asleep.

It was when I had put myself in the way of a bargain with Joseph Phipkin, owner of the *Flower of Gloster,* that I ventured to lead the conversation back to where my thoughts of gypsies were still waiting.

There is no frame of mind so conducive to an amicable interchange of ideas as when two men have settled a matter of purchase to their liking. Both are warm with the virtue of having given, both secretly with joy in that they have received. Had it left but a shirt to my back for the journey, I should not have grudged Mr. Phipkin the price he had asked for the *Flower of Gloster.* And had I broken her nose against the first bridge I met, then, thinking of the price he had received, doubtless he would have been philosophical. There was no such thing as a treaty between us. The

money left my pocket with that ease and familiarity with which money
always treats me. Judging by the way his fingers closed upon it, it found
its way into his purse in much the same manner. There are men who
spend money in this world; there are men who receive it; and the two are
always coming together over the question of a bargain. Business would
be a more ugly affair than it is if such were not the case.

'And, now that's settled,' said I, 'where am I to look for a man? I want
a man and a horse.'

'Are yer particular?' he asked

'Needs must,' said I; 'not only to the devil's driving.'

He let that pass, still waiting for my answer.

'I shall get more to the manner of the thing,' thought I, 'as I go along.
The sooner I am outside Oxford, the better.' The fact of the matter was,
that window-cleaner had upset all my balance of men and things.

'I'm particular,' I went on, 'that he's kind to his beast. Nothing else
worries me.'

'Well, sir, they're all that,' said he, 'a man don't quarrel with his bread
and butter, 'less it ain't cut to his liking.'

'I'd sooner have your observation,' said I, 'than half the learning in
Oxford.' And that being the kind of remark one makes to a man when
one is in a good humour with the world in general, he took every syllable
of it to swell himself with pride.

''Tain't no good,' said he seriously, 'going about this world with yer
eyes shut. What I say is, if a man has to be thrown amongst men it's no
waste of time if he tries to understand 'em.'

'It's a policy,' said I, 'that applies not only to men.'

'I'd do the same with wild beasts,' he replied.

'And even there,' said I, 'it might be to your advantage.'

'I can well believe it,' he returned seriously, for I had but to say a thing
with a straight face and he took me promptly at my word. 'But about
this man,' he continued. 'What yer want is some decent fellar with a
horse, what'll look after yer goin' through the locks. That's how I take
it.'

I complimented him on the gift he had of a ready understanding.

'Well,' said he, 'I've no time to waste puzzlin' out what people mean. If
my understandin' ain't good enough to take their meanin' first go-off,
it's no good my doin' business with 'em. Now the man yer want is
Eynsham Harry. He's not working just now – won't be for more than a
month. But he knows the canals blindfold – been a-boatin' all his life.
Born on a barge – he'll die on a barge, too. He's a dark-looking fellar; but
you'll find all these people are dark – dark hair, dark eyes, that browny
sort of skin, winter and summer. It ain't the sun.'

Now, this was just the point for which I had been waiting; for
whatever may be written of places, their greater interest is the people

who inhabit them. So you make a home, by those who dwell in it. When, then, he spoke of their complexion, I let him go no further.

'Has the bargee any definite origin?' I inquired. 'Does any one know where he comes from?'

He shook his head. He shook it wisely, as though much were to be said upon a matter to which as yet he had not given the fulness of his attention.

'They're not like ordinary people, anyhow,' said he – 'I've studied

them here and there, and I've noticed that. They're all dark – a brown-eyed lot, I call 'em. Yer see, they never 'malgamate. They fruitify amongst themselves.'

'Of course, if they do that ——' said I.

'Well, that's the way I understand it,' he replied.

Now, I would not have disturbed his understanding for the world, and, so far as it confirmed my ideas about the water gypsy, I was constrained to be satisfied. Undoubtedly they are of Southern extraction. Their dark, black hair, their olive skin, that soft expression of lethargy in the eyes, all point to the blood of some race other than the fair-haired Saxon. Perhaps vagabondage is in the blood and these are the outward and visible signs of a grace that I for one would not be sorry to count amongst my virtues, always supposing I were able to talk in the plural about such matters.

There was one thing more, however, upon which I needed enlightenment. The name of the man he had recommended had a touch of the uncommon about it. I asked him if it were a nickname.

'Not exactly,' he replied. 'The men are named here by the places they hail from. What his real name is, I don't know. He's probably forgotten it himself by this time. Harry's his name, and he comes from Eynsham.'

'And where shall we find him?' said I.

With a throw of his head in its direction, Mr. Phipkin indicated a public-house called the Nag's Head.

'If yer ever want a bargee in Oxford,' said he, 'look for him there.'

And without doubt this was the soundest piece of information Mr. Phipkin had yet given me.

VII

THE BARGAIN
— OXFORD

Over an affair of this nature, when the question of payment is invariably left to so much of a sense of honour as you care to lay claim to, it is as well to open the proceedings as far from the matter in hand as possible.

In reply to my suggestion, the landlord brought in whisky and water to the little parlour of the Nag's Head, where I have no doubt private transactions have taken place ever since the canals were opened. It is an old inn. The floors are strewn with sawdust. The benches are well-worn and polished. Through the door from the bar comes the sound of thick laughter, heavy voices, and the brittle clink of glasses. One glance within reminded me of the drinking-houses along the quay-side in Marseilles. In a shadow three men were playing cards with a pack whose nearly every feature had been defaced by the grimy hands through which they had passed. In the corners, men stood in groups and talked. Every man talked. No man listened. But this always happens when men are gathered together for the sole purpose of drinking.

In our little parlour it was just the reverse. Each one of us wanted to listen while the other talked, for a man scents business no less readily than he does danger. A certain flavour of it is set free from the situation; and, have you but the slightest sensitiveness to such things, you must get wind of it at once. When, therefore, such a case arises, it is wise to say as little as possible.

Now of all the men I have ever met who were keen to the susceptibility of such a moment, Eynsham Harry was the most acute. With a slow but steady eye upon Mr. Phipkin, he listened attentively while that gentleman portentously explained the meaning of my presence in the parlour of the Nag's Head.

'Harry,' said he, 'this gentleman has taken the *Flower of Gloster* for a month. He's goin' to do a trip over the canals.'

Eynsham Harry nodded his head in silence, and for a moment his eyes met mine, though they quickly fell again as though, under the circumstances, I might be sensitive to his scrutiny.

'I'm on some fool's errand,' thought I, 'and the man is sorry for me. But in this world such things may easily happen without one being sorry for oneself.' His glance in no way disconcerted me, and, after it, we

drank our whisky for a moment without speaking. Had it been a meeting of the council of ten, we could scarcely have been more serious over it.

Presently Mr. Phipkin broke in again.

'This gentleman wants a man and a horse, Harry,' said he – 'do you think we could find 'em?'

The point of the matter was now coming home to him. I wanted a man and a horse. Obviously he was the man. He had a horse as well, and for the next month was doing nothing; whereupon he became more cautious than ever.

'I've no doubt,' he replied at length. 'Does the gentleman want to find 'en in Oxford?'

'I want to start away to-day,' said I.

He shifted his cap and scratched his head.

'How about Jack Leamington?' asked Mr. Phipkin, and, under cover of his glass, he dropped a wink to me.

'Jack's all right,' Eynsham Harry replied; 'but I don't know what the gentleman wants to pay.'

'A pound a week,' said I; 'I'll find the man's food – the horse's too.'

Mr. Phipkin looked at him as one who would say, 'Now's yer chance!'

But in the light of things as I see them now, this was only a stage in the business which, for myself, I would gladly have completed long ago. But I find they like these methods. It is the one thing British about them. If a deal is to be made, there is always joy in the heart of them over the odd penny that remaineth. That glance of Mr. Phipkin's was merely to assure me that he was acting wholly and entirely in my interests. Eynsham Harry took no notice of it.

'Jack Leamington,' said he, 'would want nearer two.'

'Well,' I asked, 'supposing you were able to come, what would you want?'

He looked surprised. You would never have supposed it could have entered his head that I might suggest such a thing.

'Well, sur,' said he, 'I should leave that to you.' And by the tone in his voice it was understood that not only was I a man of honour, but of no little generosity beside.

Now by this time I had had enough of bargaining and, when you get into that frame of mind, it goes hard with you if you don't get what you want. For, I take it, in a bargain, one man at least desires to effect an exchange; and the other, if he cares little what happens, is in far the better position of the two.

'I'll give you thirty shillings,' said I, and, swallowing the rest of my whisky, I put down the glass with a rap upon the trestle table.

For yet another moment he was silent, as though a thousand calculations were passing through his mind. But when I made a movement to be off, preparatory to shaking the sawdust of the place from my feet, he clinched with me at once.

'I'll take it on,' said he, 'for a month.'

That is the best of leaving these things to men of honour. They are always fools. One pound a week would have paid him handsomely. I notice, however, that there is no such thing as discount on the price of experience. Another time I shall know better.

VIII

THE BEGINNING OF THE JOURNEY

When once your provisions are aboard, your passes signed and paid for, there remains nothing but to hitch your horse to the tow-rope and be off. Here, on the canals, there is no tide to hinder any man. At such an hour you start, because at such an hour before nightfall, when all the locks are closed, you need to be in such and such a place. Indeed, it is the life of a gypsy. Your home you carry with you wherever you go, moreover there is not one upon the road who may lift his hand to stay you.

At a quarter past four that afternoon in May, I sat in the stern of the *Flower of Gloster* and watched the tow-line tauten, saw the water-drops shake from off the sodden rope that glistened like a twisted thread of silver in the sunlight, and felt that first faint movement of the barge as she swung round into her gentle, gliding pace.

I pushed the tiller over hard a-starboard, and out went her nose into the canal's centre. One by one the ripples gathered and lengthened on the water, and soon we were leaving the towers and roofs of the old grey

town behind us.

Some twenty yards ahead upon the path walked Eynsham Harry with his horse, the tow-line sagging and tautening, sagging and tautening, as she strained or lingered on her way.

Once I lifted my head and looked above me. The sky was just beginning to tinge with primrose.

'Now, were I in London,' said I, 'my ears would be filled with the shrieks of a thousand motor horns and I could scarcely see the sky for the housetops. What is more, I'm going into a new world where never a soul will trouble to tell me the way.'

And then, as though to make the silence more absolute and complete, a peewit rose and swept in circles round the meadows. 'Pee-wit!' she cried; 'pee-wit!'

'It is little sounds,' thought I, 'that fill the silences.'

For silence is a vessel that may be filled, or may be broken. Now in London we have nothing save the shattered fragments, which not even the long sleep of a winter's night can mend. But in the country, the song of a lark will fill the pitcher to the brim. Add but the notes of a thrush, and I have known it running over.

IX

JOHN AIKIN AND ANNA LÆTITIA

The first canal to be opened in England was that in 1761, called after the Duke of Bridgewater. Since then, over 14,000 miles of navigable waterways have been brought into service in England and Wales, and scarce a soul is there, but those who work upon them, to know anything of these broad and often beautiful roads – great highways into the heart of the most glorious country in the world.

"Tis obvious,' said I, when I had read this paragraph again, 'that an Englishman has written here. But if his country be not the most beautiful in the world to him, then it goes hard with a man to find beauty anywhere.'

Those peasants in the wild mountain villages of Switzerland would doubtless find too much of Nature's gentleness in the long, low stretches of open country that lie across our land. But if Nature has been gentle with you, then gentleness is her greatest beauty in your eyes. For myself, I know I would sooner have the sweep of the open meadows, the tinkling music of the running streams and the song of a soaring lark, than all the grandest range of mountains in Europe. But then I am not a Swiss, and Nature herself has looked to it in the selection of my parents that I should appreciate what she has seen fit to give me.

Let that be as it may, I would not for a kingdom have missed those few weeks in the heart of England, far distant from any of those main thoroughfares where the dust of motors powders the face of Nature till she is worse than some painted thing. Scarce a soul is to be met along those winding tow-paths, for you may be sure that where a canal runs from one town to another, that is the longest way it is possible to go. Why, between Banbury and Napton Bottom there stands the little village of Wormleighton – a crown of old red houses upon the crest of a high green hill, – which thrice and again you circle round before you make one mile upon your journey. Now this is not the road a man would take from choice, and miles you may go, winding and ever winding through the sleepy level of the meadows, with never a human being to bid you good-night or good-morrow.

Such are the canals of England to-day. They will lead you through the quietest villages, the most remote of hamlets, with which, to know all the thousand little clusterings of people, a man might well spend his lifetime and learn but half of the country in which he lived. Indeed, men of research and patience have devoted their years to its knowledge, and at the end of threescore years and ten have offered to the press a scarce exhaustive study of just the county in which they were born. Such is good work for one man to do in a lifetime. And through these countless places, hidden in the nooks and crannies of England, the *Flower of Gloster* bore me gently, at her peaceful, sleepy pace.

So long have the canals been made by now, that but little if any of the signs of their making remain. Only for their tideless waters, many of them might well be rivers – threads of silver on which are strung the brilliant emeralds of many meadows.

I can well believe that in the days of their inception they must have seemed the work of Goths and Vandals in the land. Indeed, I find a book upon my shelves – the *Miscellaneous Pieces in Prose* of John Aikin, M.D., and Anna Lætitia Barbauld – in which these two amiable collaborators vent their united spleen upon what they call the evil Genius of the Canal.

Published in 1792, this little book of essays ran into its third edition, by which I gather that John Aikin and his companion, Anna Lætitia, had a large circle of friends. I can conceive no one buying the book but in the cause of friendship. But good or bad, it was thus far interesting to me in that it wrote of canals at so early a date.

It is written in the first person and represents the sentiments of John

Aikin or Anna Lætitia – perhaps of both. I like, anyhow, to think that it was Anna Lætitia. I will tell you later why. She describes herself, on a pleasant evening succeeding a sultry summer day, as being *invited by Nature* to take a solitary walk.

I am sure it was Anna Lætitia.

Making her way through the fields and meadows, she comes to a valley where run both a 'small meandering brook' and 'the Duke of Bridgewater's canal.'

'The firm built side of the aqueduct suddenly opened' – and here I take quotation from the book itself – 'and a gigantic form issued forth, which I soon discovered to be the *Genius of the Canal*. He was clad in a close garment of a russet hue. A mural crown, indented with battlements, surrounded his brow. His naked feet were discoloured with clay. On his shoulder he bore a huge pickaxe, and in his hand he held certain instruments used in surveying and levelling.'

Perhaps, after all, it was John Aikin.

This description, however, serves to show you the Genius of the Canal – a spirit with thoughtful looks and features harsh. The *Diety of the Stream* rises from the brook to meet him. Now, the *Diety of the Stream* is habited in a light green mantle – 'the clear drops fell from his dark hair, which was encircled with a wreath of water-lily, interwoven with sweet scented flag.'

With a contemptuous look and in a hoarse voice, the *Genius of the Canal* addresses the Brook in stern and opprobrious terms.

'Hence, ignoble rill!' he begins, after which it were not courteous to the imagination to quote the rest. Such a beginning can come to no good end. Concluding, he demands the homage – 'due from sloth and obscurity to grandeur and utility.'

To which the Brook replies in gentle accents:

'I readily acknowledge the superior magnificence and more extensive utility of which you so proudly boast; yet, in my humble walk, I am not void of a praise, less shining, but not less solid than yours. The nymph of this peaceful valley, rendered more fertile and beautiful by my stream; the neighbouring sylvan deities, to whose pleasure I contribute, will pay a grateful testimony to my merit.'

Oh, surely it must have been Anna Lætitia. I cannot conceive of John Aikin writing this. He was of too coarse a mould.

Whichever of the two it was, a strange note of prophecy is struck in the end on the Brook's reply.

'And when thy glories, proud Genius!' – so it runs – 'are lost and forgotten; when the flood of commerce, which now supplies thy urn, is turned into another course and has left thy channel dry and desolate, the softly flowing Avon shall still murmur in song, and his banks receive the homage of all who are beloved by Phœbus and the Muses.'

At a time when railways were not even dreamed of, this was indeed prophetic. But desolate though the Thames and Severn Canal now may be, it has such beauties as I shall ever remember. Were Anna Lætitia to stand at the topmost lock of the Golden Valley, where the Sapperton Tunnel pierces its dark way into the very heart of the hills, were she to stand there to-day and look down that wonderful valley of glorious gold, where in the month of May the deep woods have laid down their royal carpet of blue-bells, she must indeed retract all of that little miscellaneous

piece of prose she wrote one day, a century ago, when John Aikin perhaps had gone abroad to attend a burial, and Nature had given her gentle invitation to the fields.

X

WHY I WOULD LIKE IT TO HAVE BEEN ANNA LÆTITIA

This is why I would like it to have been Anna Lætitia. One makes pictures in one's mind; one makes them often from the books one reads. Most vividly there live in my sight the places and the people in the Arabian Nights. No artist, however skilful, could ever change my view of them. I know Herr Teufelsdroeckh as well as I know my own father. I should recognise both as readily in the street. But it is the same with every single one of us. We all have our mental pictures, and the reality can never utterly thrust them from our minds.

Now, my picture of Anna Lætitia was not conceived in my own brain. It was made for me; and if it was John Aikin who wrote the apologia, then I am all at fault and my picture is not true. But I want it to be true. It amuses me to think it is. And this is the picture – a little triolet, by Frances Cornford.

'O why do you walk through the fields in gloves,
Missing so much and so much?
O fat white woman whom nobody loves,
Why do you walk through the fields in gloves,
When the grass is soft as the breast of doves,
And shivering sweet to the touch?
O why do you walk through the fields in gloves,
Missing so much and so much?'

I am quite sure it must have been Anna Lætitia. And when Nature invited her to take a solitary walk, she put on her best white cambric, her black gloves, and off she went.

Why, of course it must have been Anna Lætitia!

XI

SHIPTON-ON-CHERWELL

Through Port Meadow the canal winds out of Oxford and, until you be past Wolvercote Bridge and Lock, there is little but the sight of those suburbs which are growing like some unsightly fungus around the larger towns of England. That people now, and more and more, should live outside the towns in which their business lies, is in no way to be regretted, but that the property should fall into the hands of those jerry-builders – men of execrable taste, whose only thought is to build for the profit it will bring them in a life-time – this, surely, is a matter for considerable remedy.

With infinite care and trouble we preserve our old buildings; why not with equal care regard our new?

The fact of the matter is, this is the age of the individualist. A man no longer builds a good house that it may be a pleasant home for his children and his children's children after him. He makes a dwelling which shall serve as profit to himself for just so long as he lives. And it is this instinct of the individualist which, amongst other things, brings about the cheap ornate style of architecture. A man builds a house to catch the vulgar eye. But in days gone past they built simply, because they would build well. A castellated turret is no fit design for a house with a rent of forty pounds a year. At such a price no castellations could be made to withstand the destructive power of time. But with a castellated turret, a residence will twice as soon be let, and so the best and simplest of labour is thrown away upon these abominable appurtenances which only degrade the taste

of those who see and live in them.

I remember well, one Mr.——, a jerry-builder in one of the suburbs of London. He threw up rows of villas in a night, as you build a house of cards upon a nursery table. One day I visited him, and was shown into the drawing-room of his own villa – the last and most ornate of a long and vulgar row.

It was papered in a bright and bilious yellow. The chairs were upholstered in plush of rich maroon – a green cloth was upon one table, while on another stood a palm in a pot bound round with scarlet crinkled paper. To complete the last expression of his taste, there was in one corner a drain-pipe of a sky-blue glaze supporting another palm, and prominently upon the yellow walls were two photographs – enlarged to life-size – of himself and his wife. Without one colour of exaggeration, this was and is the home of the jerry-builder – the man who caters for the individualist.

'You're very comfortable here,' said I, as he came into the room, his hat pitched back upon his head.

''Ere?' said he; 'well, we don't use this room much 'cept Sundays, when my daughter plays to us a bit on the pianner. It's too nice to use reelly, yer know.'

'I should feel inclined myself,' said I, 'to keep the door locked on it always.'

'I know what yer mean,' he replied, 'it *is* too good for everyday use; but after all, if yer can afford to buy nice things, I don't see why yer shouldn't be able to enjoy 'em. Nice wallpaper, ain't it? I can let yer 'ave some of that at' – he paused, doubtless to put on the halfpenny –'at one and ninepence ha'penny the piece.'

'That's marvellous!' I exclaimed.

'What – the price?'

'No,' said I, 'the paper.'

He said he knew I had good taste, and that was why he had offered it to me.

Now this is the man who has had the greatness thrust upon him of making modern architecture. The fire of London rid us of the plague. What a range of conflagration should we need to rid us of the jerry-builder!

Until you make Wolvercote, then, you will see his handiwork at every turn of the canal; but after that comes the rich broad country. Then the willows begin to draw down to the water's edge, bending and stooping like thirsty cattle to drink their fill. Their twisted fantastic roots dip deep into the cool water. I never wonder when I see a group of willows that Arthur Rackham should find them to shape into a thousand fairies and dryads. Indeed, there is a personality in every tree – a giant in the oak, a ploughman in the elm, a princess in the poplar, a knight-errant with his plume and armour in the pine; but the pollard willow, she is the home of the water sprite, the dryad and the nymph. Every branch is a fairy's arm with tapering fingers, playing strange music on the pipes of the wind.

For the first hour or so out of Oxford, I thought surely I had come on a fool's errand.

'My God,' said I to myself in despair, 'Anna Lætitia was right!' and, putting both hands to my mouth, I called out to Eynsham Harry.

'Is it like this all the way?' I cried.

He left his horse. She stopped at once to nibble by the hedge.

'Is the canal like this all the way?' I asked him as he came back along the path.

'Oh no, sur,' said he: 'look you, there's fine country soon as you come past Thrupp.'

'And where shall we stop for the night?'

'Well, that's as it likes you, sur. We reach Shipton Church 'bout seven this evening. There be a good flow of water under, and we shall make Shipton Church 'bout seven.'

'Right away, then,' said I. 'Go along as fast as you can till we get away from these damned red brick villas.'

By which you may see I was mildly endeavouring to live up to the

reputation of the bargee – a reputation for strong language which, so long as I have known him, he has utterly failed to fulfil.

'I suppose you like the old houses best?' said Eynsham Harry as he moved away.

'I do,' said I: 'don't you?'

'Well, sur,' he replied, 'I don't know that it has much to do wi' me, anyway. I couldn't stop in a house, look you; I should catch cold the first night. 'Tis the same wi' any of us used to living on the boats. I haven't slept out of a boat since I was born.'

Indeed, I can well understand it. These small cabins on the barges are as snug as they can be. A panel of one wall lets down, meeting across to the other side, and there is your bed as comfortable as that in many an hotel. When swung up again, the cabin is easily capacious enough for two, though often with these families it will accommodate more. In the same fashion as the bed, the door of a cupboard lets down to form a table. At the foot of the cabin steps, with chimney protruding through the roof, a small stove provides all that is necessary for warmth and cooking. Not an inch of the space is wasted. There are cupboards everywhere for clothes, crockery, and everything you need.

As I took the tiller again and we swung off once more into the centre of the road, I heard the old clock ticking softly in the cabin below me. At that moment the birds of one accord had ceased their singing, and except for the even, monotonous stepping of Eynsham Harry's horse, this was the only sound in all the stillness.

At Thrupp we came to the first of those drawbridges which the mere weight of a man will raise to let the barge pass through. At first I thought Eynsham Harry would never be there in time to swing her up for the barge's passage. But they know to a moment, these men – as well, indeed, they should – how long it takes. Not one instant, neither too soon nor too late, did he leave the horse's head. With sagging tow-line she walked calmly on, crossing the bridge after him to the tow-path on the other side. Then, almost as the nose of the *Flower of Gloster* passed into the shadow, he had caught hold of the big arms, lifted himself off his feet, and up swung the bridge like a feather lifted on the wind.

These bridges are characteristic of Oxfordshire. You meet with them in no other county than this. They join, as often as not, the low-lying meadows which the canal intersects, and are mostly set down with their great arms stretching upward to admit of the access of cattle from one field to another.

Immediately after passing that at Thrupp, where there is a little cluster of old Oxfordshire cottages and a farm, the canal takes a sudden, almost rectangular turn. Here it leads in a straight reach down to the church of Shipton village, which stands upon the river Cherwell.

In reality the canal is nearer to the village than the river; but in the days when Shipton-on-Cherwell received its name, they knew of no canal, nor dreamed of its existence.

It was here, in the long rushes that grow under the broad elm trees, that we moored the *Flower of Gloster,* and Eynsham Harry took the horse over the bridge up into the village to find her stabling for the night.

XII

SHIPTON-ON-CHERWELL – *continued*

In the vale of the Cherwell lies the little village of Shipton, the first hamlet of interest you will come to out of Oxford. The graveyard of the church rises from the canal's edge, and at the top of the high mound – a hill it were foolish to call it – stands the church with its square Norman tower under the deep shadows of thick elms.

There I spent the first evening of my journey, and for many a year shall remember it. It had been one of those long hot days in May when the sun in a blue heaven has warmed the ground and all the water beneath its rays. A hatch of fly had come out upon the canal and, as the sun set, while Eynsham Harry was away in the village, I seated myself on the cabin roof of the *Flower of Gloster,* watching the low-flying swallows feed from the surface of the water.

Up from the bridge, down to the corner they sped and back again. Their flight was like that of some arrow with steel-blue head, shot low from its cross-bow. Dipping on the surface, they rose again, leaving faint ripples that spread into ever-widening circles as they melted into the smoothness of the water once more. Just as this, might an arrow ricochet off the water on its flight. Then, as they swerved upwards to the turn, I caught the swift warm gleam of pink upon their throats. As swiftly it vanished when they dipped again and flashed by me once more.

Someone told me the other day that the modern aeronaut finds much to criticise in the flight of a swallow.

'With that construction,' says he, 'the swallow should not be able to fly as easily as she does.'

I have no doubt that this may be so. It is conceivable that, built as she is, the swallow should by no right fly so beautifully. But if aeroplanes be the proper method of flying, then I know as little of aeronautics as must God have done when first He made the swallow. One day, perhaps, I shall meet the flautist who will tell me that the white-throat which sang to me all that evening in an elder tree upon the other bank has no conception as to how to produce his notes. And doubtless he will be perfectly right as well. We know so much nowadays; so much more than ever we did. Look at my window-cleaner at Oxford! I am sure that Lairs and Penaits was not the full extent of his knowledge of the dead languages. In fact, I should think the only thing he did not know in this world was how to clean a window. And you can rub along quite easily without this accomplishment – especially if it be your trade.

I am content, however, with the flight of a swallow. I even approve of those few unvaried notes of the white-throat which over and over again she sang to me that evening from her elder tree.

It must have been well-nigh an hour I sat there before Eynsham Harry returned. And if I sat quite still, the wagtails came fearlessly down from the bridge under which they were a-building. They were more busy than I have ever been in my life. I thought that then – what amazing industry there is in all Nature! It is only man who, having measured out Time upon the dial of a clock, knows how to waste it; and I rather suspect that that invention of the chronometer has been his downfall. The moment he discovered that he could divide a day into hours, he began to temporise, and the first clock that rang its chime heralded the birth of procrastination. It is this way, with his endless wisdom, that a man is always making his own Frankenstein.

But in the animal world there is no other time-keeper than Necessity. Now, you cannot temporise with that. That is why the wagtails worked so hard, stepping swiftly with their dainty feet over the light surface of the mud. That is why the swallows never ceased their flying to and fro the canal. When I thought of it – all that day they had been upon the wing! Such tireless labour, if he could but achieve it, might make the threescore years and ten of a man more worthy of its record when his day had reached its end.

'I am tired,' some man caused to be written for his epitaph – 'I am tired of all this buttoning and unbuttoning.'

That he should have unbuttoned at last to so good a purpose as that truthful jest, excuses him of much of the time he wasted. But there are many of us who button and unbutton every day with no greater purpose to ourselves and others as just serves to keep us in the bounds of decency. But what is a day of decency to one hour slipped away? The swallow obeys that Nature which has been given him and earns no criticism from any one of us. Why, even on the canals, where circumstance makes no allowance for it, the ordinary so-called laws of decency are held in no regard. And no sense of yours is violated then.

I spoke of this matter one day to Eynsham Harry – I spoke of it with some reserve, yet spoke of it because I wished to know.

'What do the women of the barge do in such cases,' I asked, 'when you are miles from any cottage or place of habitation?'

'Do?' said he. 'Why, look you, sur – that hedge which runs along by every tow-path. If Nature couldn't grow enough leaves on that hedge to hide a sparrow's nest, it ain't no good to God, man, nor beast.'

I wanted no better answer than that. Where there is Nature there are no

laws of decency. Not only to the physiologist, but to Nature too, all
things are pure.

XIII

SHIPTON-ON-CHERWELL – *continued*

Seeing that one of these fine days I must lie buried somewhere, and it
being best to speak of such things while one has a voice in the matter,
then of all places let me lie under the shadow of the elms in Shipton
churchyard.

It rises in a sudden slope from the canal's edge and surrounds the
church on the crest of the mound. In the early part of May, when first I
visited it, the high, thick grass was dotted with cuckoo flowers from the
midst of which the moss-grown grave-stones just rose in unobtrusive
memory of those who lay beneath. Nearly all the raised mounds of earth,
often so sadly reminiscent of the shapes of the bodies they cover, were

concealed in the long grass; but where one was exposed, there lifted the scarlet head of a tulip as though to prove how full of life is that acre which belongs to God.

When I returned in the last week of the month it was all changed. From the plain, pink muslin of her cuckoo flower, spring had put on her gorgeous lace blossoms of heracleum. The whole place was white and feathered with their blooms. Scarcely above them, then, rose the silent heads of the grave-stones. Often you must push the blossoms aside to read the names of those who lay beneath. And above it all, like a sentinel guarding the peace of those good country folk who slept there, the tower of the old Norman church rose out of the thick branches of the elms and faced the sky.

> 'When the night comes for me to rest,
> Let me lie down in the long green grass.
> I need no garden with fine flowers dressed
> When the night comes for me to rest;
> Where Nature sows I shall sleep best,
> And where God reaps no place surpass.
> When the night comes for me to rest,
> Let me lie down in the long green grass.'

At Shipton House, which stands just next to and above the church-yard, they told me that once King John had had his garden. Dr. Yule, who lies buried in a vault beside the church, has no doubt written of this in the papers he compiled concerning the history of Shipton. I called at the vicarage there, in the hope of being allowed to see them, but the vicar was at Oxford for the day, and, writing later, he was possibly still away in Oxford, for I received no reply. In any case, it is not wise to let valuable papers out of one's hands, and that to the first vagabond who happens to come along.

As I walked up the drive to the vicarage door, there were some jolly children playing on the lawn white with daisies. A little dog left his frolicking with them and came to tell me that I was nothing less than an intruder.

> 'Hark, hark, the dogs do bark,
> The beggars are coming to Town.'

That little nursery rhyme ran inevitably in my head as I rang the bell. Of course, the vicar was quite right not to answer my letter.

But if he had, I might have written more of the history of Shipton, of which I am assured there is no little to be told. And yet, this is no guide-book, so perhaps it is as well without. I only loved the place as I saw it with its elm trees and its cow-parsnips – the old Roman cross that stands solitary in the grave-yard, and all those wild flowers of the field which combine to make it one of the most restful spots I have ever seen.

For some hours that night I lay awake listening to the great silence. No doubt it was the first strangeness of that bed in the cabin of the *Flower of Gloster* which kept me from sleeping. But it was a rest to lie there, nevertheless. Through the open doorway of the cabin the stars were glittering in a deep-blue sky, and now and then a bird chirped sleepily as

its mate pressed close against it on the branch.

'A man might do worse,' thought I, 'than spend his life like this.' But when I began to consider how it might be done, I fell asleep.

The next morning we started at five. I was sitting on the roof of the cabin eating my breakfast as we passed through Heyford Lock.

XIV

SOMERTON

All that day we wound through the meadows. The cattle came down to the water's edge to look at us as we passed. They were shy, curious things, young heifers. The world is very new to them. In their soft eyes is all that patient wonder of the child. So near did we pass them at times that, had I swung the tiller round, I might have touched their noses with my hand.

So the day slips, just as the meadows pass, in that silent, gliding way whereby it is gone before you have thought to count an hour of it. Only now and again is the pleasant monotony of it broken by the commotion of a passing barge. Then there is cracking of whips, the raising of voices, the soft scraping purr as the boat runs by you, touching your side. Scraps of conversation are exchanged ere they shoot out of distance and, turning some sudden corner, are lost to sight. For a long while before, you may often hear them coming. Where there is none to lead the horse, a man will sit at the tiller with his whip, cracking it ever and again as the gentle beast lingers to nibble from the hedge. Nearer grows that sound and nearer, until the smoking funnel from the cabin fire can just be seen above the hedgerows. Then round she swings into sight – a Fellows Morton with a load of straw, a pair of Falkeners with cargoes of best bright, or a Shropshire Union with her odorous merchandise of gas-water.

Sometimes perhaps it is a fly-boat out of Birmingham, travelling her steady three miles an hour, day and night, like the old express coaches of a time that few of us are now left to remember. One and all they know each other's journeys, as sailors will tell you in mid-ocean the destination of some passing vessel; as ships too, they will hail each other in passing while the tow-lines swing across.

'Good morning, Joseph!'

'Good morning, Harry!'

'If 'ee see Sam in Oxford, tell 'en I've got that there horse for 'en whenever he wants to see 'er.'

And then no doubt may follow little scraps of canal gossip in voices rising as the distance increases between them. For never do they loiter. Time is a precious matter with them, and with them also necessity is their chronometer. They are like the wagtails. Often I envied them the hours they spent a-working.

At Somerton that second day, I had lunch at a little inn by the canal side; indeed *I* might loiter as I chose. It was while the good lady was making ready – the boiled eggs, the glass of beer, the piece of cheese – that I strolled up into the village with its grey stone cottages and neat, trim gardens. A Norman church is here as well. Eynsham Harry came with me, and together we secured the keys. A youth of twelve, of a

suspicious turn of mind, was deputed to carry them and accompany us.

For a moment I stood looking at the Tower before we entered.

'Nine hundred years old seems very little when you look at that,' said I.

Eynsham Harry stood and stared at it.

'Is it nine hundred years since that was built?' he asked presently.

'It is indeed,' said I – 'there or thereabouts.'

'Well,' he added after a pause – 'I 'old wi' churches in their proper place.'

But what he meant by it, I cannot attempt to say.

By this time the boy was waiting at the door, and in we went, whereupon the boy followed us closely, watching all we did. I fancy he was more deeply suspicious of me. I think, moreover, he was right. With a rich and a poor man, I would always mistrust the rich. There is only one reason why a poor man steals – the pain of extreme need.

Beyond that, there is nothing so honest as poverty. Now, of the two of us, my poverty was the least apparent. It came, no doubt, of having a coloured tie, a gold watch-chain, and a crease to my trousers. It was not a crease that lasted for long; but this was only my second day. I have no doubt, however, that Eynsham Harry is a richer man than I am.

When I found the youth at our heels in the chancel, I turned on him.

'What are you afraid we'll steal?' I asked.

'There be'ant nothin' to steal,' he replied – ''tis all lockit up.'

I asked him why, and he told me that two weeks before an old silver chalice had been stolen, by visitors, from the altar. I can conceive no theft more meanly done than this. One might never say a prayer in a church from one year's end to another and be little the worse for it; but to steal from the high altar – were it only a flower at harvest-time – must be the greatest of all deadly sins, whether it be included in the seven or no.

But this guarding the stable when the horse was locked up somewhere else was characteristic of the precaution of country life. I could not help but smile. The boy followed our every footstep, and the moment we had gone out locked the door again, taking the coppers I gave him with a pull at his forelock.

Back at the inn where we had lunch, I found a book, the title of which attracted me. *A Book on Etiquette, by a Member of the Aristocracy.*

'Is it etiquette,' said I, 'to announce in print that you are a member of that much-to-be-envied class of people?'

Eynsham Harry set a piece of cheese upon his knife and shook his head.

'Let's see what he has to say about it' : whereupon I opened the book and read.

'When entertaining guests,' says this member of the aristocracy – or it is words to this effect – 'do not produce the family album and expect them to be interested in portraits of people whom they have never met. Rather keep them amused and interested by light and chatty conversation, so that they will feel the time pass easily until it is the proper moment to take their leave.'

I wonder how many trusting people have taken to heart these words of a member of the aristocracy, putting away their splendid albums wherein the photo of Uncle William taken in Toronto in a violent thunderstorm always made everyone laugh who looked at it? I wonder how many dull evenings that member of the aristocracy is accountable for, when the poor hostess strives a thousand times to begin a light and chatty conversation and, failing utterly, falls to silence, yet still refrains from bringing down that leather-covered volume with its nickel-silver clasp?

It is not fair when you are a member of the aristocracy to take such advantage of your power as this. There is only one thing to be done. Let some honest merchant in the suburbs write a book and call it a *Book on*

Sincerity by a Member of the Democracy. Only it would never repay him, and I am sure that book on etiquette was a gold-mine.

XV

THE TRADE IN OLD BITS

'Ride-a-cock horse
To Banbury Cross
To see a fine lady on a white hoss.'

Indeed you must say – hoss. There is scarce a child of any discrimination who would listen to you if you did not. I wonder – without any of that sentiment about it at all which so many people dislike in others and enjoy so much in themselves – I wonder how many little pink fingers have been pinched, how many little crumpled toes have been pressed to the concluding lines of that well-worn nursery stanza? Many and many a million, and doubtless there will be many a million more.

That was indeed a literary achievement to write but one stanza which, for so many centuries, should be sung to the race which is to be; a stanza, moreover, bringing with it those wonderful echoes of youth to every grown-up man and woman who inevitably repeat it to themselves whenever they hear the name of Banbury Town. It may have been of political significance once. So far as I know, the real history of the rhyme has never been traced. But the women of England have found other uses for it, and I am sure they know best.

We came into Banbury that evening where, leaving the barge to Eynsham Harry, I went up into the town. He needed to go no further than some public-house such as the Nag's Head in Oxford. There are always inns ready to the canal to supply the needs of the barges passing continually backwards and forwards. I left him there and hurried up into the town before the shops should close.

There is little of the old aspect of Banbury left now. Agricultural advancement – as indeed with advancement of any sort – has set upon it the seal of the new order of things. A few of the old houses remain; a few of the old inns. Old arches beneath the houses will often invite you to stop and look within; but as often as not they are disappointing. The Reindeer Inn still has its beauties. The shop in Parson's Street dating at least, so I am informed, from the year 1616, still sells the famous cakes made from the old recipe, and still keeps the odour of its years about it. They even retain the old windows, just as they were, against all the tempting advantages of plate-glass.

The new cross which stands in the market-place was erected in 1858 to commemorate the marriage of the Princess Royal with the Crown Prince of Prussia. I do not think it pretends in any way to be a copy of the old, or even to occupy the original site. It is two centuries and a half ago since the Puritans destroyed it. I often wonder where vandalism ends and religious zeal begins. It must be a fine line indeed that separates them.

But were I bent upon giving a history of the Town of Banbury or of any other place upon the road, this chronicle of the *Flower of Gloster* had never been written. What happens to you upon a voyage of discovery is that you learn the world by what you see and not by what you hear.

Indeed I saw little in Banbury, for, to tell the truth, the cross greatly disappointed me, and neither appetite nor curiosity were strong enough to persuade me to the cakes. Beyond these, is there anything in Banbury but legend and fairy-tale? There are numbers of windows filled with the glaring modernity of agricultural instruments. No doubt they have grown into their place in the field; they have become part of the soil upon which they work. The whirr of the reaper is now a sound that one has learnt to associate with those still, hot days of late summer. It is as natural to the ear now as the note of the corn-crake. I would not lose it for the world. But, displayed as they were in the streets of Banbury, I felt them somehow out of place.

As I stood and looked at them, I thought of that farmer in the south of Ireland, when first he brought the reaper and binder into his fields. He had only hired the machine. So delicate and intricate an instrument was beyond his means to buy. He had only hired it, and stood there in his cornfield with me as slowly and surely it narrowed down the swaying army of blades of wheat. I watched the wonder in his eyes as the

relentless arms swept down their burden against the knives, as, load by load, they gathered it into sheaves, bound it and cast it from them. For a long while he never spoke. He watched it silently with a breathless interest – a conscript thrust unwillingly into the invading ranks of time.

At last he turned to me.

'Shure, 'tis the divil in ut!' said he. 'Mind ye, 'tis no surprise to me the way ut reaps at all, but how the hell does ut tie the knot in the shtring? There must be fingers to do ut – faith, 'twill take me all me time to tie a knot meself, but that damn thing does ut wid its eyes shut. I don't like the ways of ut at all.'

That was just what I felt when I saw the agricultural machines in Banbury; but it was the looks and not the ways of them I disliked. And that was not the only thing which spoilt my impression of the Town. I went to a curio shop there. Where, indeed, did I not go into a curio shop? In most of them is that inimitable atmosphere of age. The world has a history to it in these places; but in this curio shop there was none. All the brass candlesticks and bed-warmers looked unreal.

'Is this old brass?' I asked of the man who served me.

'Every bit of it,' he replied with confidence.

I picked up a box, purporting to be one of those old candle boxes which have come to us from Flanders.

'This old?' said I.

'Oh – yes – oh, yes,' said he – 'we don't touch anything but old bits.'

I examined it, and found that the hinges were new. The solder joining it together was as fresh as paint; the very edges were sharp. No hands had ever lifted that lid when the long winter evenings were drawing in. No tallow candles had ever lain there waiting to be used. It was all redolent

of the agricultural machine, and there was no soil of which it could become a part.

'How much do you want for it?' I asked.

'Twenty-five shillings.'

I smiled. In Birmingham where it had been made, probably it had cost two. Now, when he saw me smile, thinking too perhaps from the way I had examined it that I knew more than I really do, he made a generous, nay, a flattering offer.

'Twenty shillings to you, sir,' said he.

'You know it's not old,' said I. 'You know it was made last week with seventy others in Birmingham.'

'Had it eighteen months myself,' he replied.

I replied that it was older than I thought; but still I pressed my point.

'But you know it is not really old,' I persisted.

'I believe its made up from old brass,' said he.

I laughed. I could not help it. I laughed aloud at that.

'Why – my God!' said I, 'all brass is old – as old as the metals from which it is made, since they're as old as the earth they come from. Made up of old brass! Now, supposing I hadn't known any better, would you have let me purchase that believing it to be old?'

'Why not?' he replied. 'If you hadn't asked, why should I have told you?'

'Then I take it,' said I, 'that your idea of the truth is the contradiction of a lie. You must tell your lie first.'

'Whose telling lies?' he demanded.

'Well – one of us,' said I, 'is telling the truth. I shouldn't like to hurt your feelings by saying which of us it was.'

He followed me to the door with the old bit in his hand. I don't think I should care to be a trader in old bits. The world is so full of fools, and every fool is a temptation to a would-be honest man.

XVI

CROPREDY

It was after leaving Banbury that the interest of the journey scarcely ever faltered. Had I really known what travelling was until I went aboard the *Flower of Gloster?* I scarcely think so. The member of Parliament in the early part of the last century who complained that it was a tempting of all Providence to ride upon any vehicle exceeding the speed of twenty miles an hour, has all my respect, if so be it he was speaking of travelling. This insensate desire to get there takes all meaning from the verb "to travel." Indeed, in these days it would seem that the only effort of a man is to conquer the dimensions, to annihilate Space, to crush Time beneath his heel. For man is becoming a socialist not only in matters political; he would deny even the monarchy of Nature, dethroning that by which alone he may come into his kingdom.

But in the name of Heaven, what has this to do with barges? Yet, if a man must travel from London to Birmingham in a few odd number of minutes, let him at least once in his life take a barge from Oxford and do it in five days. It will teach him much, and, amongst other things, he may find that the dimension of Time is not to be conquered by beating.

We started late out of Banbury that next morning. I must confess it, I lay long in bed, and not all the sounds of other barges slipping their lines could waken me.

When at last I did get up, I gathered from Eynsham Harry that the other boatmen had been laughing at him for the strenuous labour of his journey.

'They say you'd make a fine master for a fly boat, sur,' he told me.

'One man's meat,' said I; 'but it's past belief that any man could find this life a poisoning, even if he were to travel night and day.'

'Well, sur,' he replied – and here I learnt he had by way of a philosphy – 'men have peculious ideas of how they shall enjoy themselves, and they most ways signifies what sort of men they are. 'Tis one man in a thousand as chooses in this world what he shall be, but every jack one of 'em select their own enjoyment. I had a week in London once, and there was a friend of mine what spent every evening going to a theater. I've never thought properly of him since.'

I thought softly of the times that I had been to the theatre, but said no

word of it. I share that weakness in common with many, that at all
hazards I would be thought properly of. Moreover, there was a note in
Eynsham Harry's voice which made me feel that, in what he said, there
was a point of view which it might take more than logic to destroy.
There was more than the Nonconformist conscience to it. I doubt, in
fact, whether it were a matter of conscience at all, for he was not a man to
be worried much by trifles.

'Well, how,' said I, 'do you find your enjoyment?'

He was taking the tiller, making his morning ablutions at the same
time, while I lay stretched upon the cabin roof. Fanny, the horse, was
ambling quietly along the tow-path, just keeping the line from sagging in
the water whenever I had the energy to crack the whip.

Eynsham Harry dried the soap-suds out of the corners of his eyes
before he answered me.

'Well, sur,' he replied, 'as I said before, what I calls enjoyment another
man may find little but a waste of time; but, look you, so long as it
enjoys me, where's the call to fret about it? If I've got any time on me
hands just about this season of the year, I can't do no better with myself
than go birds-nesting.'

I had thought of – oh! I had thought of everything but that.

'Birds-nesting!' said I. 'Have you got a collection of eggs?'

'No, sur – I had when I was a boy. When I was a youngster I used to
think there was no sense in goin' a-nesting, not unless I took the eggs. I
don't touch 'en now.'

'Why not?'

'Well, 'tis all right in young fellers. I don't stop my son a-doin' it. But
if he takes more than one egg out of a nest, I give 'en a thrashing. 'Tis all

right with young fellers. They want some sort to boast about. 'Tis proper for them to have the feelin's of competition. But, God bless me, I don't mind if a man knows more about birds 'n what I do. All I feels is I'd be damn glad to have a talk wi' 'en.'

'So you get just as much amusement in finding the nest, though you don't touch the eggs?'

'Every bit, sur. I came back last Sunday week, and I said to my boy: "Sunny," said I, "I found a red-start's nest this morning – four eggs." "Where, dad?" says he; "I haven't got a red-start's." "No, not in your collection," said I, "but I've got four in mine. And you won't learn nothing about the ways of that bird – not if I tells you where her nest is. 'Taint no sense in buyin' eggs. You find 'en, and then you'll know something you didn't know before."'

When a man makes you think, there is more than just something to him. From this moment to the end of the journey, I never regretted that thirty shillings a week which had been cajoled out of me in the private parlour of the Nag's Head. Had it been but to learn just this one characteristic of him, the thirty shillings were worth it.

For some little while, then, I sat looking on ahead to where Fanny was quietly making her journey. Every moment she would shuffle a step nearer to the edge, casting a wistful glance at the young, green shoots of the hawthorn. Another step nearer, and at the crack of my whip she would fall back into the tow-path's centre with a dropping of her ears, well knowing she had been found out.

'Then I suppose,' said I presently, 'you don't like London?'

'I do not, sur – there's no Nature in the place. 'Tis all people. And I holds when you get all people and no Nature it ain't natural. 'Tis Nature what gives us something to be doin', and when you've got none of it, then people invents their enjoyments out of their own heads. I've heard tell they do queer thin's in London. I've heard tell there are women at the theaters there what dance wi' scarce no clothes on them, and that people come in thousands to see 'en. I've heard they go putting themselves into positions as any woman would feel shame to be seen in, and that ladies go wi' gentlemen to watch 'en. Now, look you, sur, they wouldn't do that if birds built nesties in London.'

The amazing amount of truth in so preposterous a statement almost bewildered me.

'You go up to London,' said I, 'and say that where people can hear you.'

''Tis no affair of mine, sur,' said he quietly. 'They ain't my children, or I'd thrash 'en.'

I laughed. I pictured Eynsham Harry thrashing the countess of ——

'But it's a strange thing,' I went on presently – 'you know the boys of the present generation are losing all their interest in Nature. The modern

school-boy no longer spends his half-holidays in birds-nesting. There's scarcely one of 'em knows anything about geology. Collections amongst the school-boys now are matters of business. They collect stamps only to sell at a profit. We're becoming worse than a nation of shopkeepers. We're a nation of pawnbrokers now, pledging everything we have for the sake of an appearance of wealth. I've watched the boys at Wellington College. When they come out of school for their half-holidays, they go straight away to a hosier's shop and buy the latest thing in socks, the smartest thing in ties. They go to the barber's and get their hair neatly trimmed and scented. Why, I remember when I was at school, if a boy had scent on his hair, my God, he never forgot it!'

'I don't know nothin' about that,' said Eynsham Harry. 'I never went to school myself.'

'But you can read and write?' said I.

'Not a word,' said he. 'All those poster things on the hoardings as we come into Birningame mean nothin' to me.'

'I've always thought,' said I, 'that there were many drawbacks to education. Then you know nothing of what you should add to the homely salutation of good-morning?'

'No – good-morning is enough for me,' he replied.

'It should be enough for anyone,' said I.

At this moment, while he was looking in the cabin mirror, brushing his hair, I took the tiller and straightway, being more concerned with our conversation than any matter of steering, I ran her nose full tilt into a built-up side of the bank.

'By God,' said he with a laugh, 'that gave her Warwick! It only shows you, sur, that we must have been talkin' very foolish.'

It was quite pleasing, that childish sense of fatality. There was the best of Calvinism in it.

A moment later we took a sharp turn under a bridge, and there were the black arms of lock-gates stretched out to greet us.

'What place is this?' I asked as I saw the cluster of red-tiled roofs that spoke a village.

'This is Cropredy, sur – Cropredy Bridge. We'll just get through the lock and stop a bit. I always go here to the Red Lion for a drink.'

XVII

THE FIRST PATCHWORK QUILT – CROPREDY

To the Red Lion we went, leaving the *Flower of Gloster* moored by the bank on the far side of the lock; giving Fanny her nose-bag, for which she made a pair of big dark eyes blink gratefully.

These country inns with their floors of sawdust, their old lead-lighted windows through which the sunlight falls and makes the floor a chequer-board of gold, they always delight me. It is here of an evening you learn something about the land you live in. The boards of the trestled tables bear the ill-cut names of many a one who has laid down the law and told the Prime Minister in a few straight words just what he thought of him.

In the middle of the morning, when the men are away working in the fields and the parlour is empty, what a place to sit in, to call for a glass of beer, a plate of cheese, ere you set forth again upon the journey you may be taking! To some inns there are small gardens set out with their patchwork of flowers. Where they face upon a street, as did the Red Lion of Cropredy then, as often as not a jug of flowers stands out upon the window-sill. They are a patchwork collection, too. Country people never put one kind of flower in a vase by itself. They mix them all up – roses and daisies, Canterbury bells and geraniums, all are thrust together in one multi-coloured mass. That is their idea of colour – a patchwork. They know nothing of chromatic scales, of tones that blend or harmonies that meet. They mix their flowers as they see God mix His. That is good enough for them. It is a patchwork.

It was an old woman far away in the heart of the country, as you may fancy, who first thought of a patchwork quilt. No artist could ever have thought of that. It was an old, old woman with a twinkle of laughter in her eye and a child's love of colour in her heart.

One day, when first she was wed, she burnt a hole in her red flannel petticoat. It was only a small hole, but when she picked up her skirt to cross the road on a muddy day, she felt all the neighbours' eyes upon it. So she cut a square piece out and stitched another in. There was that neatness about it, you could never have seen where it was done.

Now what was the good of the piece she had cut out? None at all! But it was excellent flannel. If you want to know the truth of the matter, she had bought that petticoat for her wedding morning. Wasn't it a pity to throw it away? Well – she saved it.

That was the birth of the patchwork quilt.

Along with that piece of flannel, which was tucked away in the deep corner of a drawer, there was added a square piece out of the seat of her husband's trousers. And so, piece by piece, increasing in numbers as the family increased, the material of the ultimate patchwork quilt was slowly harvested in that drawer. But what she was ever to do with them, that she could never have said. Necessity decided that for her; for it was Necessity who is the greatest craftsman amongst men.

They grew old and they grew poor. And as they grew old, they felt the chill of winter the more; and as they grew poor, they had not clothes sufficient upon their bed to warm them.

It was then she thought of her pieces that now filled the recess of that old drawer. Necessity whispered it in her ear and, picking up her needle, she began to sew. In a week the patchwork quilt was made; and in the early mornings when they lay awake, in all her seriousness her husband would point out a patch to her and say:

'Mother – where di that coom from?'

'That,' said she, 'were the tail out of our Johnny's first little shirt.'

This is one of the beauties of a real patchwork quilt. For these are the things that really keep you warm.

XVIII

THE RED LION – CROPREDY

Almost from the canal's edge a little street runs up, with a row of Tudor cottages on one side and the high wall of the grave-yard on the other. This is the village of Cropredy. A few outlying houses there are, of course, a farmstead here, there the vicarage; but this little street is Cropredy. Down this street the horses of the Cavaliers galloped one day with a brave rattling of harness and the wind in their plumes. You cannot but feel that little has changed since then. Only the canal is there, which in those days was never dreamed of. But so long has it been in existence now, so long have the barges been passing to and fro, that even that seems part of the place.

It is in the midst of this row of cottages that you will find the Red Lion. To the gentlest breeze, a red sign-board swings outside, adding another instrument to the orchestra of sounds which are inseparable from the country village. I wish to hear no better music than the symphonies which Nature plays upon her countless instruments.

When we walked into the parlour, two farmhands were already there. On their way from one field to another, they had chosen a path which must lead them through the village; and the sign of the Red Lion had swung backwards and forwards, singing its song of invitation. Where is the man who would not have stepped within? Their pints of ale were on the trestle table. The sun was shining a rich amber through the rough glass mugs. Their arms, bared to the elbow, were burnt and brown. The sawdust of the floor never looked so clean.

'Good mornin'!' said they – 'a fine mornin'.'

What club is there in London where a man, if he did not know you, would say as much? What club is there would provide the entertainment we had there then?

Upon the wall opposite the open fireplace there was a board, marked out as a sun-dial, each division bearing the value of some number. A ring in the centre marked the highest number of all. The board was painted black, and all about the face of it were little holes where darts had entered. It was a game they played to while away a lazy hour.

At Eynsham Harry's invitation, we played with them then – played for four glasses of ale, while the landlord in his apron leaned within the doorway, keeping the score with a piece of chalk, pleasantly content whoever won or lost.

And the glass of ale that followed! I can see the sun sparkling in it now. Each one of us as we raised it to our lips muttered 'Good Health' – and not only wished, but felt it.

Is there any club in London where, upon your first entrance, old members would treat you with such good comradeship as this?

For every meaning of a club, there is no place to touch the village inn. Here a man upon his entrance is straightway at one with all the company – a good fellow until he proves that he is not. A gentle thirst is the only qualification for membership, and it black-balls no one. Not a rule is written, but every law is tacitly obeyed. A man expels himself. There is none of the terrible formality of compulsory resignation. If he is not liked, he does not enter the club. He condemns himself. It is only the hyper-civilised conditions of modern life which make these things impossible. In the city you must make your rules and print them; but in the country, they take their laws from Nature, the book of which is spread open in the fields that those who run may read.

XIX

THE HISTORY OF CROPREDY

Had I meant to be chronicler of anything beside my journey in the *Flower of Gloster*, doubtless I should have left the history of Cropredy alone. But the best of a chronicle of this nature is that you may set out with one intention and, before you have gone a mile or more upon your journey, find yourself in passing company with another.

To speak of the history of any place is much in the spirit of the guide's litany; but when I sat alone on the lawn of the vicarage garden and read the brief history of Cropredy from the papers which the vicar was good enough to give me, I said to myself, 'This is not wonderful – it's true.'

There are no astounding figures of height and breadth and depth, therefore I have no desire to astonish you with the year of our Lord. It is the year of our Lord – if you will have it so – 1911, and the village of Cropredy has been asleep for two hundred and sixty-seven years.

Two hundred and sixty-seven years ago, they fought the battle of Cropredy Bridge. But even two years before then, the king's standard was set up at Edgecot, and all around Cropredy, in the meadows, the king's army slept the night before Edgehill.

I should like to have been sitting that night in the parlour of the Red Lion. I would have liked to have heard the songs of the Cavaliers as they heralded the coming of the morning.

'King Charles! Who's for a fight now?
King Charles! Who'll do him right now?'

The greatest poet of the last century knew well the lilt of them.

But it was two years later, in 1644, that Cropredy heard the music of the clash of arms, the thunder of battle. Eleven cannon and fourteen small brass and leather guns were taken on that day. And Colonel Weymes was made a prisoner. You have only to stand on Cropredy Bridge, with the meadows at either side of you, to see it all; you have only to walk up the cobbled pavement in the little street to know what a day that was in the history of Cropredy.

Even now, they still dig up cannon shot, soldiers' buttons, and rusty swords when the blade of the plough throws back the secretive earth. In the churchyard itself there are two tombstones bearing each the inscription, "A faithful soldier of King Charles ye First." Indeed, the next day after the battle – so the records of the church will inform you – it was the vicar's duty to bury five soldiers. Only these two of their tombstones remain.

I think I should like to be a vicar in some country parish in England. The peace and quietness of those vicarage gardens, walled snugly off from the old church, are ideal corners of the world. It must, too, be a great thing to tell people what you think of them, at least once in every week; to sit at ease in your own garden with every flower that you can wish for, the old gardener cutting the grass of the lawn to the somnolent whirr of the mowing machine, and there compose a stirring sermon against the venial sin of idleness, sipping your glass of cider as you round a well-turned invective against the increase of drinking at the Red Lion or the Glass Bottle. I am sure I should like to be a vicar, if only for ten days, so long as they had two Sundays in them.

I enjoyed that hour in the vicarage garden while I sat upon a deck-chair on the lawn; I enjoyed it as well as any spent upon that journey. Maytime in a garden is the best of all the year, for a hundred flowers are blooming and all the roses yet to come.

'I don't care,' said I to myself as I sat there, 'I don't care who says ought to the contrary – it's good to be alive; and were I the most intellectual pessimist in the world, I would sooner be a brainless optimist if it lost me the pleasure of this day.'

I remember a man once saying to me, "Optimism is the last resource of the pessimist."

And as is always the case, when a thing sounds very clever I am at a loss to reply. At a moment like that, it must be something still cleverer, or nothing at all, and in common with most people I am much better when I say nothing at all.

But by the time I had sat down to think about it, I came to the conclusion it was not so clever after all. It was the cry of the pessimist who would be an optimist if he dared, but would never dare for fear of lessening his intelligence in the eyes of others.

I thought of this little epigram that morning as I sat in the vicar's garden. I expect I smiled as I recalled the face of the man who had said it – pale, tired, the face of one who is awake only at night, the hair long and interesting. And from thinking of that, a song came into my head – a flight of fussy sparrows across the lawn no doubt had put it there —

> ''Twas in the merry month of May,
>   When all the birds were choiring.'

What is more, I sang it. There was no one about. I thought I sang it quite well.

XX

THE SPARE BOOTLACE

We had left Cropredy a little more than an hour, when Eynsham Harry stood still upon the tow-path and pointed across the meadows to where the canal wound under one of the countless bridges.

'Look you, sur,' said he, 'that bridge on there by the third bend.'

I nodded my head.

''Tis called old town bridge. I don't know how many years it was ago, but once there was a town there, and a war came what blew it right away. Leastways, that's what they tell me.'

I turned and looked at the sloping meadows, spattered with daisies and with cowslips. A score or so of young heifers, white and ruddy brown, were peacefully grazing there; a few starlings were hovering near them, timid with all their fearlessness to get their food. It seemed impossible to think that a bloody, decimating war could bring about such languid peacefulness as that.

'What was the name of the town?' I asked.

'I don't know that, sur. I only know there was a town. Sometimes now, I hear, they dig up things in fields – pots and the like, of what they used to use in the old days. But would you ever think it, sur, to see those fields there? They be filled with larks' nests now.'

''Tis ever the way,' said I – 'one world builds upon another. How do you know that there are larks' nests there?'

'Look up in the sky, sur.'

I looked. Three larks were soaring, infinitely high. Their ceaseless music fell to us like fountain drops of water.

'Their mates are on the nest,' said he, 'and there be a hundred more of them resting in the grass. 'Tis a fine part of the country this for birds. I've found sedge-warblers, reed-warblers, and black-headed buntings down by the banks of the canal, and there, up in those woods, 'tis full of all sorts.'

'Let's come up there now,' said I, 'and see what we can find. I haven't looked for a nest these eighteen years.'

He needed no other word to persuade him, and, tying Fanny to a post by the old town bridge, we set out across the fields in the direction of where the village of Wormleighton with its crown of trees stood high upon the hill surveying all the country round.

On our way to the wood we crossed a country road. Upon a bank of grass by the side of the ditch sat a pedlar eating his lunch, a crust of bread and meat. He was only a pedlar in bootlaces and imitation flowers – conventional roses, red and white, cut out from small turnip heads, the red ones stained with cochineal. A certain craft there was about them, a certain simplicity which just saved them from the bathos of their foolish wooden stems.

He held them out, and I stopped to look at them. It was then he told me how he cut them out of turnip heads.

'Me own idear, sir – I've never come acrost any as does the likes of 'em. Me own idea hentirely. I've made these for sixty years.'

'How old are you now?' I asked.

'Seventy-three, sir.'

'And still tramping the roads?'

'I don't arst nothin' better, sir.'

'And are you always travelling in the same goods?'

'Well, I varies 'em a bit – studs sometimes, then back to bootlaces, then garters for the girls, then back to studs again.'

'But you always sell the roses?'

'Yes, I find they go – always. 'Tain't no good tellin' a lie about it, but I sold the first of them to the Duchess of Kent, the old Queen's mother.'

'I am glad to see you tell the truth about it,' said I.

'Well,' he replied, 'I find it pays.'

I walked away.

'There are some tricks,' said I to Eynsham Harry, 'that are so cheap as can pay no man to work them.'

Now, from the moment I had said that, I felt my conscience in reproach against me.

'But I am no fool to be taken in by a ruse of honesty such as that,' said I to myself.

'A pedlar must take the world as he finds it,' said my Conscience.

'And must pay for his mistakes,' said I, 'as a tradesman allows for his bad debts.'

Now, a Conscience, if you be fool enough to keep one, is a very woman for the last word, to whom, if you would be on your best behaviour, you must stay and listen whether you like it or not.

I thought I had got safe away with that last retort, but the fiend of my Conscience was quick to assure me that had I nothing but a grass bank on which to sit, a piece of bread and meat for food, and that begged at a fellow-creature's door, I might stoop to meaner measures than this pedlar.

I had by this time had enough of it. The distance between us was getting greater with every step, the penalty to pay to my Conscience harder with every moment.

'If I don't turn back now,' said I to myself, 'I shall never do it at all, and make a bed-fellow of this fiend for the night.' Whereupon, I said I had suddenly thought of my need of a bootlace, and, hurrying back, left Eynsham Harry there upon the road.

'I want a bootlace,' said I to the pedlar.

With a ready hand he pulled it out from his bunch, and what I gave him my Conscience has more account of than have I.

''Tis the ways of one man,' said my Conscience, as I walked back along the road, ''tis the ways of one man to tell the truth to keep his pride, while another tells a lie to save his face.'

''Tis no lie at all,' said I, 'for every man on a journey of this nature must need a bootlace and to spare.'

It was not more than three days later that I had to fit it into my boot and, calling my Conscience to account of it, found that she would not answer me. Now, isn't that a woman all over?

XXI

SCHOOL-DAYS

'There's one thing,' said I, when I had joined Eynsham Harry again, and we were making our way across the fields once more to the wood, 'there's one thing where your idea of enjoying yourself falls short.'

'And what's that, sur?' he asked.

'Spring gone, and you're done for.'

'And how's that, sur? There's more to learn of a burd than just where she lays her eggs. She has her young to rear through the early months of summer; she has to teach 'en to fly; she has to teach 'en the best places where they'd most like find their food. She has to live herself through the winter. I've watched the burds here along by the canal; I've watched 'en when the snow was four inch deep along the tow-path, and all these fields were a sheet of white with never a foot-mark on 'em. And look you, sur, not that only, but the branches of the trees and all the hedges with never a leaf on them, white too, every inch, wherever the snow could settle. Well, now, sur, if courage is a sort of thing you'd like to think about, you'll see plenty of it then. There's a look in a burd's eye in winter, sur, as I wouldn't care to have to see in any child of mine.'

'What sort of a look?' I asked.

'Well,' said he, ''tis as if the hand of God, as I heard a parson say once, was lifted against 'en. I've known 'en settle on the barge as we went along, so driven was they to look for food. Yes, sur, I think birds is the most couragious creatures there is. Why, do you know, one day a fly-boat came along the five-mile pound between Marston Doles, top of Napton Locks, and Griffin's Bridge at Wormleighton here. She was a steamboat, and was making up for time over the five miles. I suppose a spark must have flown out of her funnel and set fire to a little bush where a thrush was sitting on her young. Anyhow, when I came by, I found the bush all charred and burnt, and all that remained of that poor little burd, still sitting on her nest, burnt to a cinder. She'd never left 'en, not when the flames was all round her. I haven't heard nothin' better'n that, sur, for courage – man or woman.'

'Do you know the notes of all the birds?' I asked presently, for the relation of that little incident would have demanded some moments' silence from anyone. Such a tale you do not hear every day.

'I'm gettin' to know 'en, sur, but it takes me longer'n 'twould most people. I've no more ear for music than my horse, Fanny, has. She knows the crack of a whip, and that's about the only note she'll dance to. I'm little much better myself, and I don't suspose I should ever have taken to study the notes of different birds if hadn't a' been for a gentleman I saw one evening standing on that swing bridge we passed goin' through Thrupp afore we came to Shipton-on-Cherwell. He was standing on the bridge there, and I had to ask 'en to get off so as for the

boat to pass through. "Fine evening," said he as I came up. I agreed wi' 'en and asked 'en was he looking for fish, for he'd find a sight more of them in the Cherwell. "There's a pair of reed warblers," said he, "built in those rushes last year; I was listening to know if I could hear 'en now." "Wouldn't it be better to see 'en?" said I. And then he told me 'ow 'e's sight was so bad he could only just find 'is way about and, being interested in burds, 'e'd learnt all their notes. But then I made out afterwards, sur, that he was an organist in one of these churches you'll find about the country. 'Tis an easy matter for him. I'm getting it meself, but it's a slow job. D'you hear that now?'

We stopped and listened. Amongst all the sounds of birds and insects, I could detect one incessant note. How I knew that that was what he meant, I cannot say; but I was sure of it. It was as when one bids you to listen to a sudden movement in a symphony, and through all the instruments of the orchestra you can detect the notes of one violin, never rising above, but stealing through the harmonious melody of the whole.

'I know that,' said I – 'it's a chiff-chaff.'

He looked at me very steadily for a moment or two.

'If you know more about burds than what I do, sur,' said he, ''twould be kind of you to say so. I've no want to be making a fool of myself before no one.'

I laughed.

'You needn't be afraid,' said I. 'I used to know them when I was a boy. It's more the school-days coming back again than any knowledge of birds.'

Upon this we had plunged into the woods, and, by the time I was half way up my first tree, with Eynsham Harry standing there below me, those days were all come back again. It might have been a half-holiday and I a boy of ten.

XXII

POUR PASSER DOUCEMENT MA VIE

I remember, amongst the old china in the Musée Cluny, finding a bowl of that simple design which, you must know, had many years ago belonged to one of simple tastes. It was of green-white china, and upon the inside, in letters of blue that I cannot possibly forget, but could not match were heaven dependent on it, were written the words, *Pour passer doucement ma vie.*

It is often a little thing like that which lives in the memory.

I thought of it again when we reached the little village of Wormleighton. Here indeed is a corner of the world where I could wish gently to pass my life. But I shall say that a hundred times of many another place before this chronicle be ended.

It is the Manor House at Wormleighton where I could wish to spend the rest of my days. A fine piece of Elizabethan architecture it is. Indeed, it may well be older than that. I would not ask that any should rigidly believe me when I talk about architecture.

For the mere trouble of signing one's name in a book, the present owners are magnaminous enough to let one see within. I wondered should I be as generous if it were mine. A stranger seeing over your house is the pure essence of intrusion. I hate the sight of him, even when I would wish to let and welcome him as a possible tenant.

Yet I felt grateful enough to be shown over the Manor House at Wormleighton. In September of 1571 the Earl of Leicester with a brilliant retinue stayed there on his way to meet Queen Elizabeth at Warwick. She

too, upon her progress from Edgecote to Warwick by way of Long
Itchington, she too slept the night there ere she passed on to meet her
Leicester.

But it is the memories of Prince Rupert which cling closest to the
place. There you may still see the Star Chamber where he dined the night
before the battle of Edgehill.

'There is one panelled room,' said the little maid who showed me
round. 'Would you like to see that?'

I said that indeed I would, and straightway she took me there.

Before we entered, she knocked softly on the old oak door. A voice as softly from within bid us enter. The little maid opened the door, and there, in no large room, but panelled to the ceiling in warm, brown oak, sat an old lady by the mullioned window, a sewing basket upon her lap and in her hands a piece of embroidery through which her needle glittered and disappeared, glittered and disappeared to every movement of her skilful fingers.

Never in my life have I felt such an intruder as I did then.

She bowed to me and I bowed to her.

'It's very beautiful,' I muttered foolishly.

'It is indeed,' said she, and fell to working at her embroidery again, never dreaming that I had meant not only the panelling; never dreaming that in that word beautiful I had included the glimpse of the old garden outside, and above all herself. Indeed the panelling was wonderful, the garden was wonderful too. But it was she who made the picture. I shall remember her when all these other things have gone out of my head.

In another moment I had thanked her, excused myself and retired. And as I walked down the passages into the garden once more, those words on the old bowl in the Musée Cluny came softly back into my mind – 'Pour passer doucement ma vie.'

XXIII

THE HEDGEROW PHILOSOPHY

Soon after Wormleighton, we passed the last of those Oxfordshire bridges which make so characteristic a feature in all that meadow landscape. Onwards from there, through Marston Doles and Napton, it was scarce worth one's while to travel.

I sat disconsolately on the cabin roof and hoped for better things, but they did not come. We passed no village of interest then. It seemed as though the canal had wilfully sought deserted channels. For the first few corners that we reached, every hope I had rose expectant at the thought of what might be beyond. That is the best of a corner in this world. At least it promises; without which, hope might die of sheer starvation. Even a promise, broken, is something to live upon; yet there comes a time when they are but husks in the mouth. I grew tired of these broken promises at last.

'Does it improve at all between this and Coventry?' I asked Eynsham Harry presently.

He looked at me steadily, and then – which is an event with him – he smiled.

'It's very samesome, sur,' said he, 'all the ways from here to Coventry.'
'Then why did you smile?' I asked.

'Well, sur,' he replied, 'if you'll pardon me saying so, there be nothing
the matter wi' you, but that you be young.'

'You mean foolish?' said I, for it would seem that one has to be
well-advanced in years before one makes a compliment out of the
accusation of youth.

'No, sur, I said nothing so impertinent. 'Twas young I said, and young

I means. You want your cake before you've eat your bread and butter. 'Tis the way wi' my son John – "If you're not hungry enough," I say to 'en, "to eat your bread and butter first, you ain't hungry enough to eat cake." '

'I've heard that argument before, you know,' said I. 'It rakes up memories of days I'd give much to live over again. But it's not sound. It never convinced me then. It doesn't even convince me now. I've stodged myself many a time to get to my piece of cake. It only takes the gilt off the gingerbread by the time you do come to it.'

'Well – isn't that a good thing, sur?' said he. 'The cake is not so wholesome, and it costs more than bread and butter. Come a time and you'll do without it altogether.'

It is not that I am accustomed to having the better of an argument; but I felt none the less surprised that I came off so badly in this.

'Now where do you,' said I, 'who neither know how to read nor write – where do you get your logic from?'

'I don't know, sur,' he replied – and with such honesty as I would give much to meet with every day – 'I don't know, sur, for I don't rightly understand 'ee when 'ee talks about logic. I says what I thinks, and mostly I thinks what I finds. This world ain't no easier to live in, sur, for the help of luxuries. There's scarce a man finds an easier place of the world than that tramp we met selling bootlaces outside Wormleighton. They say the more you have the more you want, but, by God! it's the more you have, the less you can do without. Now, that ain't making the world an easy place to live in.'

'Then why,' said I, 'did you refuse my offer of twenty shillings a week and look for thirty?'

When a man is talking as much sense as this, it is taking no mean advantage to put such a question to him. He took it quite good-naturedly. He smiled as he thought of our bargain in the Nag's Head.

'Because,' said he, 'the more you have, sur, the more you want, and the more you want, the more you have to pay for it. When a gentleman like you comes out a-boating for little more than a holiday and offers five shillings more a week than a man expects, 'tis only right to take it that he's offered less than he's ready to pay.'

'Good Lord!' I exclaimed, 'd'you mean to say that fifteen shillings would have been enough?'

'It would indeed, sur – and I'll take it now, if so be you think I've not done fairly by you.'

I lay back on the cabin roof, and, upon my soul, I laughed.

'You're quite right,' said I. 'One does these things so often with one's eyes open, that after a time they become glazed. I remember once when I lived near Covent Garden, I used to get up early of a morning before the market closed, and I'd get Darwin tulips for twopence a bunch. Now, when I go to a florist up west, they charge me a shilling. What's more, I pay it. It's the same thing.'

'Well, I'll take fifteen shillings, sur,' he repeated, 'if so be you think I haven't done fairly by you.'

'I'd sooner give you five more than fifteen less,' said I. 'A man's philosophy is worth it any day of the week. But what I want to know is, where you learn these things. You say you think what you find; but what do you find?'

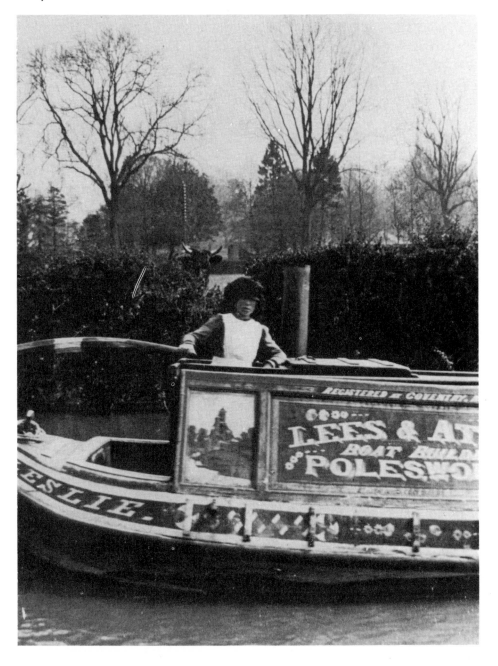

He was silent for a moment while he took the narrow passage beneath a bridge. When we had come out into the open canal once more, he turned and looked at me.

'Well, sur, last year I was coming along this very pound, and as I came by a corner down there – I was just in front of Fanny on the tow-path – I started up a hawk from the hedge. I thought she could be up to no good, so I marked the place with me eye, and at first when I came along I could see nothing. But when I went down on me hands and knees, I made out a dead field-mouse – them little creatures wi' the pointy nose, the size of a man's little finger. Did I say she was dead? She wasn't quite. The little beast was quivering. The hawk had dug her out of her hole, and there was the little store of nuts and berries she'd set by her for the winter time, all scattered about in the grass.'

' "Look you here, mother," I said to my wife. "Whenever you've got sixpence in your pocket and want to buy something you don't need, just make a little nest of it."

' "If you mean that mouse," said she, "what's the good when the hawk came and took it?" '

I echoed that good lady's sentiments to the letter.

'Had I seen that,' said I, 'it would have driven me to the utmost limits of extravagance.'

'Well, 'tis curious,' said Eynsham Harry, 'the way people do argue. If it hadn't been for that kestrel, I might never have learnt that 'tis the ways of the field-mouse to make her store for the winter months. The first thing I reckoned was that for one mouse that had been killed, there were a thousand what had made their store against winter in safety. Why, there must be hawks, sur, and hawks must live, same as Jews and company promoters, but it isn't every man as need be caught by 'em.'

'It comes to this,' said I, 'that you're the true-born philosopher. You learn your philosophy from the hedgerows. I only play at it.'

'Well, sur,' said he, 'I've often sat and looked into a hedge where all the insects be creepin', and I've said to myself: "You be near as ever you be in your life to the greatest secret in the world." But, bi God, I've never found it, sur.'

I turned away, disheartened with my own short-comings.

'Where does that branch of the canal lead to?' I asked presently. We were approaching a bridge on the right, raked over the water in a long low curve that made a picture in itself.

'That, sur,' said he, 'is the branch of the Warwick and Napton.'

'It goes right into the town?'

'Yes, sur.'

'Then let's turn out of this,' said I, 'and stop the night at Warwick.'

XXIV

WARWICK

When I saw the countless volumes showing in the windows of the booksellers, all relating to Warwick and its environs, I said, 'Not a word of the history of Warwick will I write. This voyage of the *Flower of Gloster* is a voyage of discovery. I can find nothing here but what has been found already.'

Yet what one can say of Warwick beside the relation of its history, it puzzles me to know. I was debating on that very subject as I walked up the High Street, my attention first this way and then that, yet history, nothing but the history of England, stared me in the face. Outside Leicester's hospital, a man was acting guide to a group of people, and to every word he said, their mouths, almost imperceptibly, widened in aperture.

'It's no good telling us all those names,' I heard one of them say at last – 'we shan't remember one of 'em. Just let's know when it was built and if those beams are real oak. We've got to go over the Castle yet, and by schedule we must catch the late train to Stratford-on-Avon.'

I stood for a moment to listen, and in five minutes heard the history of Leicester's hospital over three hundred and fifty odd years. When he had finished, the speaker of the group turned to one of his companions.

'Did the Morgans see this place when they were in Warwick?' he asked.

'No,' said the other. He shook his head to emphasise it.

'Well,' said the first, 'we can tell 'em all about it. Three hundred and fifty years – it's great.'

I walked on, trying to think of those three hundred and fifty years. It was impossible. I could only think of that five minutes.

A few yards down the street, a man stopped, smiled genially, and thrust out a hand of welcome.

'Hallo, Matherson!' he exclaimed jovially, 'never thought I should find you in Warwick.'

'No more of a surprise, Cubberwheat,' said I at a venture, 'than my finding you here.'

Now, I never saw anything quite so sudden as the fall of that man's expression. In one moment it dropped the full ninety degrees which lie between pleasant satisfaction and offended dignity. Matherson, no doubt, was a man whom he wished to stand well with; Matherson was a man whom he was proud to know.

'My name's not Cubberwheat!' said he emphatically, with insult ringing in his voice.

'My name's not Matherson,' said I.

'What! not Matherson of Coventry?' he asked, for if I were not Matherson of Kamschatka, he was determined to have it that I was

Matherson of somewhere.

'Not even Matherson of Coventry,' said I.

'Well – I'm certainly not Cubberwheat,' said he. 'Cubberwheat!' he added in disdain, and thereat turned upon his heel abruptly leaving me to stand in the street.

Apart from a slightly wanting sense of humour, I have nothing to say against this gentleman's pride. Doubtless his name was Jones; but whatever it was, to anyone save Cubberwheat himself, the name Cubberwheat is an insult. But it is quite amusing when you think that it applies also to the name of Jones. If I were to address Mrs. Cubberwheat – supposing she exists – by the name of Jones, I doubt if a sense of humour would save her. It would be a great one if it did.

Seemingly, not only is the Englishman's home his castle, but his name is the flag he flies to show he is in residence.

I took a furnished house in the country once, and the owner assured me, with a marked tone of seriousness in his voice, that there was a flag-staff in the garden and a Union Jack in the boot-cupboard under the stairs.

'Of course, if you have to go up to town,' said he, 'you can just put the flag back into the cupboard.'

'Then why is the rent only three guineas a week?' I asked him.

He shook his head sorrowfully, for I had signed the agreement by then.

'It ought to be more,' said he.

'Undoubtedly, it ought,' said I.

'But I hear you write books,' he added.

I admitted the impeachment.

'Well, if you like,' said he, 'you can put the place into your next book. You can use the address. I don't mind.'

'Some of my books have a very bad name,' I warned him.

'Oh! then perhaps you'd better leave it alone,' said he. 'At anyrate, here's the key of the boot-cupboard.'

I wish that more people had his sense of humour and that less were conscious of what they have.

I passed another bookshop after I had left my friend Cubberwheat. Within the window I saw volumes bearing the titles, *Shakespeare's Land, Warwick and its History, Shakespeare's Avon,* and so on.

'I'm sure there will be nothing about Warwick in my barge book,' I said to myself. And there is not.

XXV

THE GATE INTO THE BLACK COUNTRY

I had been into the Black Country before. I had driven over many of those roads through the charred heart of that desert of land, which is more like to death than the Dead Sea. It is an awful yet wonderful part of the world. God has deserted it – left it absolutely to the hand of man. And in those hands, as one might well suppose, all but human nature lies dead. All the green goodness of the earth has gone. From one mile to another there is no blade of grass will live. The very mould is black, a bed of ashes in which not even a weed could find its nourishment.

I have heard the complaint, half jest, half earnest, that the Almighty might have done things better than He has. *If I were God,* a modern author titled some pamphlet that he wrote. That, no doubt, was the jest in earnest. But you have only to go into the Black Country to know what can be done with a wonderful world when God delivers it into the hand of man.

I know very well that there is the pulse of England's greatness, that out of Bradford, Halifax, Huddersfield, Rochdale and Burnley, the stream of molten metal flows through the veins and arteries of a great nation, nerves her to face her enemies, and feeds those energies by which alone she can maintain her position in the world.

But what a price to pay, and what a coinage to pay it in! If you believe in the efficacy of war, then doubtless the Black Country will seem most wonderful to your mind. In fact, whether you believe in it or not, those belching furnaces and that poisoned land must make you marvel as you pass it by. The black sweeping hills with scrubby bushes leafless and dead; the men and women, white-faced and dirty with the everlasting falling of the sooty air; the thousand factories and the countless furnaces; the utter lifelessness in all this seething mass of life, however much he might shudder at it, a man must stop and realise its greatness.

There are two places in the world which seem like hell to me, two places which, if I had the making of hell, I would closely imitate; the one is Monte Carlo and the other the Black Country, two opposite poles, the last extremes of luxury and labour.

And here, all the year round, thousands and thousands of human beings work out their salvation. One almost asks if salvation be possible;

for not only the skin but the lungs, not only they but the heart, and not only the heart but the very soul of a people must be blackened in such an atmosphere. It seems fitting in irony, that when they take their holidays, they should throng to a place called Blackpool – a very pandemonium of amusements where for a time they can forget the sweat and labour of their daily lives. It is just forgetting, and that is all.

Now Birmingham, beside being the centre of all the canal traffic of England, is, as it were, the outer gate of all this sunless country. Why I

should have gone so far as even to approach it again, I can scarcely understand.

'If it's the country you want to see, sur,' Eynsham Harry warned me, 'then have my advice and do nothing wi' Birningame. I've seen more dead dogs and cats in the water between Knowle and Olton Bridge than ever I have thrushes in the hedges.'

Notwithstanding even this, I went, and to this moment regret the hours we wasted. From Turner's Green to Knowle, along a ten-mile pound, the surrounding country might well be worse. Then came the six locks at Knowle, up which we climbed wearily, a height, it must have been, of over a hundred feet before we reached the top. The only one of us who really enjoyed it was Fanny. Here she was given the bucket with her fodder, and for the next hour, while we raised and lowered one lock after another, munched steadily with that appetising sound all horses

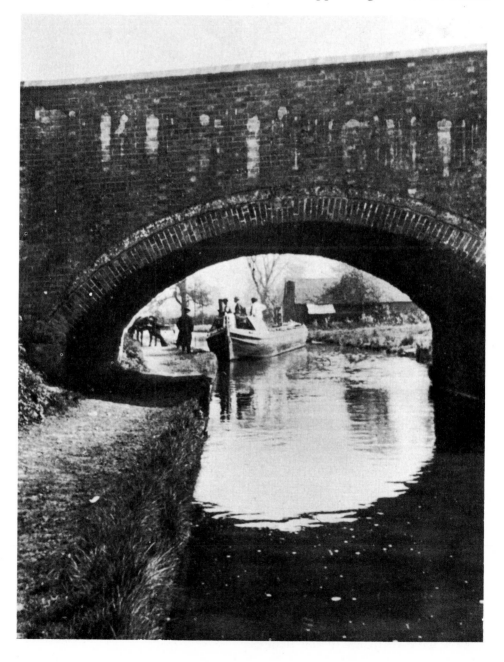

make when they are eating.

At the end of it, I caught a glance from Eynsham Harry as I stood up to ease my back; there was, as well, the suspicion of a smile in his eye.

'What is it?' I asked.

'Do you think you'd like the life a-boatin', sur?' he inquired solemnly.

'Life is much the same whichever way you take it,' said I. 'I've never met a road yet but what it had a hill to it some way or other.'

'Quite true, sur,' said he; 'and it isn't even experience will teach some

people what they can expect to find on the other side of the hill before they sets to climb it.'

Then I understood the light of laughter in his eye.

'You mean we've sweated up these six locks for nothing?' said I.

'Well, sur, there's no sweating, if he comes by it honest, can hurt any man; but you don't be the gentleman wi' the tastes I think you have, if you like your journey on from Knowle to Birningame.'

No one ever assessed my tastes so accurately. I chafed against it the whole journey; but when a man has put himself in the way of a bad bargain, he is not going readily to admit he is made a fool of. I stuck to my pride as long as I could; sat on my favourite seat on the cabin roof, and hailed with joy a bank of blue-bells which lent their colour in a deep purple to the dark reflection of the dirty water.

Eynsham Harry said nothing, but I felt that he was just biding his time till we should come to the outskirts of Birmingham. And after Solihull, they began in earnest. The ugly buildings of the labourers and artisans commenced to line the canal side. The trees and fields grew less and less in number. He had not exaggerated for a moment, when he spoke of the dead dogs and cats in the water. One after another we passed them, their milk-white swollen bodies lifting high above the stagnant water.

Even the men passing us through the locks lay inert and lifeless on their cabin roofs, as though the journey of the last few days through all that blackened country had brought them to exhaustion.

At last I turned to Eynsham Harry and admitted my folly.

'You're quite right,' said I: 'there are some hills it would be as well to learn of before one climbs them. What's the quickest way out of this?'

He never so much as showed a sign of triumph when I admitted my defeat.

'Our best way now, sur,' said he, 'would be to turn back till we come to Lapworth. There be a junction there wi' the Stratford-on-Avon canal going through Preston Bagot and Wootton-Wawen. I think maybe that 'ud more suit your fancy. 'Tis close by Henley-in-Arden, and the world's quieter there'n what it be here.'

I swung the tiller over straight away as he unhitched the tow-line.

'May I never realise again,' said I, 'how great a country England is.'

And there are many who, if they stood at the outer gate of the Black Country, would say the same.

XXVI

THE STRATFORD-ON-AVON CANAL

I never did a better piece of business than when I took Eynsham Harry's advice and turned back to Lapworth. To be quite accurate, the junction of the two canals is at Kingswood, and from there through Preston Bagot is but a matter of thirteen miles. But the waterway, as I passed along it in the *Flower of Gloster,* was deserted, and they are thirteen miles right out of the track of the world.

Sometimes, they tell me, a barge makes its solitary way down to

Stratford, but the locks have in the crevices of their gates all that luxuriant growth of water-weed which shows you how seldom they are used.

Many and many a mile of canal in England now is thrown out of service by the iron roads, which as yet have not succeeded – as also the canals, to the critical eye of Anna Lætitia – in fitting themselves into the landscape. Will they ever indeed become so intimate a part of the soil as have the harrow and the plough? Truly, I wonder what Anna Lætitia

would have to say, did she hear the thunder of the express down one of the great railroads through this very country she loved so well? Quite easily could I imagine her now sitting down at her desk to write another paper, but this time in praise of the Stratford-on-Avon canal; calling forth the evil Genius of that iron road which has drawn its fretted lines across the face of Nature, thrilling her reader thereby with the horrors of civilisation. And if in those days she abused the canal, what would she say of the Black Country now? Certainly she would no longer put on her white cambric and her black gloves. I can see her in crape and jet from top to toe.

But now from the dull crape of the Black Country we came to the meadows once more, all in their spring muslin, and such muslin as only Nature knows the weaving of. The white thorn hedges were half in bloom, the buds some green, some breaking white. That alone is a

trimming of lace which the most cunning fingers in Spain have never equalled, not even for a prince's cradle or a cardinal's robe. Here and again in the hedgerows stood a crab-apple tree, pink-white in bloom. Did they ever in France paint such dainty flowers on silk as these? And by the water's edge grew those reeds, yet young enough to keep their pale flesh-colour before they swelled into the full green of summer.

What a joy it was after the smoke and ashes of Birmingham! I lay full stretched upon the cabin roof, my face in my hands, the sun beating down upon my head, drinking it in as, in summer, the labourer in the corn-fields drinks his jug of cider to ease the parched dryness of his throat.

'How can a man care for that devastating march of civilisation,' said I, 'when it means the ultimate destruction of such places in the world as this? God knows we must progress; we cannot stop still. The mind must grow, or it will atrophy. But if ever a plant needed light in which to bear its flower, that plant is the mind.'

But this is just the way a man talks when God is in His Heaven and the complete rightness of the world is on every side of him. It is, as a matter of fact, only in the deepest tribulation of his soul that he speaks the truth; for when everything goes well with him a man has little judgment to boast about, and says the first thing which, with the lightness of a feather, rises flamboyant to his head.

I could not have found such great wisdom in what I said aloud that morning as I lay stretched out on the cabin roof of the *Flower of Gloster,* because, no sooner had I said it than I began to sing with such voice as God has given me – all the snatches of songs, every one I knew. Where I had forgotten the words, I made them up. Sometimes they rhymed, sometimes they did not. It was a happy matter of chance.

> ''Twas in the merry month of May,
> When all the birds were choiring.'

I began with that, no doubt because it was still in my head from that morning in Cropredy. In the country, a tune such as this stays with you an unconscionable length of time. You hum it to yourself last thing at night before you go to sleep; you wake up, and there it is still with you in the morning.

Now, all this is better than any philosophy. A man who can sing to himself – when, in such a case as mine, it cannot be particularly pleasant for him to listen to – is far on the way towards taking life in the easiest way imaginable.

It is surely not all a question of mating when birds raise their voices? What mistress can ever hear her master, the lark, when he sings up in those heights of air in the dim distant chancel of the clouds? I am quite

certain that even Bellwattle, whose only knowledge of music is composed of a couple of lines from the most antiquated ballads that were ever composed in the early fifties, would never have listened to me that morning for five minutes.

No; when a man sings to himself, it is because he can dispense with all philosophy. Wherefore, I did away with my speculations upon the progress of the mind. It mattered little to me then whether, like a bulb, it could grow in darkness, or, like a seed, it must have the light. All that mattered was the whole world, decked in muslin; and so I sang, with what effect I have already given you to suppose.

XXVII

LOWSON FORD

In those parts they call it Lonesome Ford. That is better than just the giving it of a good name. 'Tis as though from long association the place had named itself. It lies alone in a cup of hills like a polished pebble in the deep pool of a twinkling brook. Right through the centre of the village runs the canal under an old red-stone bridge, with the low tiled lock-house just beside it. Here and there the old half-timbered cottages are placed with but little sense of order – rough facets of the stone that glitter with colour as you look down on the village from the hills above.

There may be other villages in England more peaceful than this, but in my journey in the *Flower of Gloster* I never came across them. In towns and cities the houses can well be said to be awake. There is an alertness about the appearance of their windows; the doors open and shut with a sound that has life even in its echo. But here in Lowson Ford all men and things would seem to be asleep. The cottage windows open to the sun, the doors ajar, the gardens patient in the heat; even the farmers' waggons, with their heavy wheels and cumbrous horses, saunter through the street all as in the idle causelessness of slumber.

I would not for one moment say they do not work in Lowson Ford. I saw farm labourers coming and going from the White Horse Inn, so work there must have been a-doing somewhere. But had they been going and coming from the White Horse Inn in their hundreds, then I should only have felt that it was I who was asleep, dreaming one of those mad summer dreams when things happen, all disproportionate to what they are.

You could well spend a summer in the village of Lowson Ford and forget that the world was moving round about you. It is an event, unparalleled almost in excitement, when a barge comes through to Stratford. Then all the little boys and girls rush down the street to the old

red-stone bridge to watch it as it passes through the lock. The fat
lock-keeper's wife wakes from her long months of somnolence, bestirs
herself under the admiring eye of all the children, though she has nothing
whatever to do. Her big woolly dog, of such a breed as I have never seen
before or since, rouses himself from the sun-warmed coping stones of the
lock and follows after her, with a sense of importance, half awake,
watching her with his eyes wherever she goes. Oh, Lowson Ford, I can
tell you, is wide awake then, when a barge goes through the lock! But the

barge goes on its way into the busy world; the smoke of its little chimney from the cabin fire trails round the corner and, blue as it is, melts into the bluer air of distance. Then Lowson Ford turns on its side once more, and for many a month to come sleeps like a baby in its cradle of the hills. If ever I need sleep to wake again, I shall go and find my pillow there.

Yet even in such a place as this, so grim a thing as tragedy can find its way. But then, as you might so well suppose, it is not the tragedy of distorted face, of twisted features of the like you find in cities. The little tragedy I met in Lowson Ford had not such ugliness as made me shudder when I came face to face with it.

It was making late in the afternoon when we came there. There was that warmer colour in the sun as when it throws its light through the dust and heat of the day's journey. The whole village seemed deserted, though through the open doors of the cottages I could just make out the old women seated over their evening meal, pouring the tea from warm brown earthenware tea-pots into their big kitchen cups, nodding their heads and gossiping. Old women must talk, for Nature leaves them little else to do.

But one figure commanded all my interest, even my curiosity. He stood on the bridge looking down the canal at the *Flower of Gloster,* watching her silently as she entered the lock, crossing to the other side, still watching us in silence as we came through into the open pound once more.

Here we moored her to the canal bank and, jumping off, I came up on to the bridge to speak with him. He had that look of a man who has yielded up all his active interest in a busy world and is content to be a silent spectator of the life which passes close around him.

'If of nothing else,' thought I, 'I shall learn something of Lowson Ford.'

He looked just the sort of man who would be proud of being the oldest inhabitant. Yet he was not so old, after all.

'Thirty years I've been here, sir,' said he.

'And what age are you now?' I asked.

'Seventy-one.'

'You get the pension, then?'

'Well' – he smiled – 'I'm qualified for it, as age goes. But I've a little bit of land and a cottage of my own. I don't take the pension. I'm quite comfortable – as comfortable as I shall ever wish to be.'

He pointed to a little half-timbered cottage, just climbing up the hill. I could see the late tulips like brilliant coloured stones in the prim mosaic of the garden's flowers.

''Tis a charming place,' said I. 'If I were your age, I would not ask better than to spend the rest of my days there.'

His eyes looked very firmly out before him, and under his white beard and moustache I saw his lips set as though he were suffering a pain he would have no one know of.

'May be I'll stay there,' said he slowly – 'I haven't made up my mind.'

'You don't mean to say you're going to move?'

He just bent his head in the affirmative.

'But not into a town?' I asked.

'No, sir – no – not into a town. I lived in London once, when first I married – but – but it didn't agree with – my wife. We moved then to Basingstoke – that didn't agree with her either. Then we came here, and we've been here thirty years.'

'How long have you been married?'

'Fifty-one years.'

His eyes blinked quickly and he screwed his lips again. I had almost asked him what pain it was, when the look passed away once more and silence came beside us for a while.

'Is your wife up at the cottage?' I asked presently.

He nodded his head, but never turned his eyes to look in that direction. And then I felt impelled to notice something strange. It was more than the look that had passed across his face. It was more than the pain I thought he had spasmodically been suffering. His eyes were filled with water; but that I imagined might well be the weakness of old age. The whites of them were tinged with red. But as the strangeness of his manner impressed me, I began to think I had not read these signs aright. Suddenly I felt awkward, ill at ease. It came upon me quickly that he wished to be alone. Whereupon I asked him if he had had his tea, thinking doubtless of those passing glimpses I had got through the cottage doors as we came by.

He shook his head.

'Well – you mustn't let me keep you,' said I. 'I expect tea is your best meal in the day.'

Then he turned his face and looked at me, and never have I seen so deep a look of suffering in the face of any man. It seemed as if he knew more agony of mind than he could bear.

'I've been trying to go this last hour,' he muttered brokenly, 'but I daren't.'

'Daren't? Why not?'

'My wife died yesterday – sir – she's – lying up there in the cottage.'

Once more came silence to ease us. He leant back again on the bridge, and the muscles in his face were twitching under the thin white hairs of his beard.

There is nothing ugly in such a tragedy as this; but it is none the less great for that. I thought of the utter desolation in his mind; for many a time, no doubt, he had stood upon that bridge, watching the life of the village until the welcome hour came that called him up to tea. And now, of all the hours in his day of desolation, this was the most terrible he must face.

'I'm sorry,' I said lamely – 'I'm sorry I did not understand sooner.'

He shut his lips as he made another effort to be brave.

'That's all right, sir. I tried to tell you before, but it was difficult. It is a great parting, you know, after fifty-one years.'

I have remembered that simple phrase of his best of all – 'It is a great parting.' How great a parting it must be, I do not dare to think; for after

such a time neither a man nor a woman run their race alone, but like little children, confidingly, hand in hand.

A few words more to make our parting less abrupt, and then I thought it best to leave him. One fights these tragedies best alone.

I walked through the village then and came eventually to the barge by another way. Fanny was hitched once more to the tow-line, and we set off. As we turned the corner of the hill, I looked back. He was still there, still resting both his arms upon the bridge. He had not dared as yet to go back to his tea. What is more, I knew he never would. The late evening must creep down the village street, and then, when the shadows spread their cloaks over the things one sees so plainly in the day, he would steal back alone to his cottage and with wide eyes watch through the night until 'twas day once more.

XXVIII

YARNINGDALE FARM

Steep, on one side the canal, between Lowson Ford and Preston Bagot, the high land continues for a mile or so, and, soon after we had turned the corner, leaving the village out of sight, I took to the tow-path, walking for a while there alone by Fanny's side.

That old fellow on the bridge had brought me the need of silence and my own company. Even the philosphy of Eynsham Harry would have seemed out of place, though I have no doubt he would have had much to say that was wise upon the matter. One may not think conclusively by oneself – I am sure that I do not, – but at least one thinks pleasantly. Even that tragedy, as I thought over it alone, seemed to fill me with a sense of awe which I could not call unpleasant. I should only have found its irony had I talked of it aloud.

So I walked alone with Fanny, soothed, I have no doubt of it, by the unvarying expression of her face as she toiled monotonously along the tow-path. Often I glanced at her, and she suggested nothing to alter the even tenor of my mind. Those were peaceful days, those days on the *Flower of Gloster*.

'Sur!'

I looked back.

'Will 'ee take the tiller a while and let me get back? Look you, I forgot to get milk in Lonesome Ford. The jug's empty.'

It seemed a pity that he should have all the way to go back. I looked about me right and left. On the crest of the hill above us there was a house in the midst of a clump of elms. Apple trees blossomed near it. I could see their white lime-washed trunks. There were outhouses beside. Assuredly it was a farm.

'I'll climb up there,' said I. 'Give me the jug. That's a farm. They're bound to have some there.'

He handed it to me over the side, and, taking a gap in the hedge, I set off up the steep grass slope, still glad to be alone.

They had made the hill an orchard, and never do fruit trees offer so fine a pageant of their blossoms as when, tier upon tier, they rise above each other up a steep hill-side. And here, on the crown of the hill, in the midst of its orchard of white-trunked apple-trees spread with bloom, stood an old English farm-house, one of those places that seem to make English history a thing of yesterday. If I came across one, I came across a thousand in that journey in the *Flower of Gloster,* and each fresh place I found had all the new wonder of age to make it as beautiful as the last.

Through a wooden gate into a small odd garden before the house – where flowers grew, it would seem, more by favour because they liked the place than from any care or cultivation, – I found a path of uneven flag-stones up to the door. There I knocked, waited, and then knocked

again. There was no answer.

In the farm-yard close by, the chickens were scratching in the hay; an old cow chewed the cud under the apple-trees in the orchard. She had a rolling jaw and a calm eye, which she quietly fixed on me. As good as speaking, she told me that no one was at home. On the window-sill outside an open latticed window a black cat lay fast asleep, where the last light of the day's sun could warm her. A brood of young chickens peeped out of the bars of their coop as I still waited on the step before the door. Yet I could not believe that the place was utterly deserted. The farmer's wife would come presently. She was out at the back of the house doing her share in the work of the farm. But no – I heard no one. I looked up at the bedroom windows : they were all closed. Then, just as I was about to knock again, I realised that the open window was to my purpose.

As I stepped across to it, the black cat opened her eyes, stretched forth

her front paws and yawned. Her mouth and tongue were scarlet. A tulip
in the bed below her was not a brighter red. But she moved no more than
this, even when I leant across her and peeped into the room through the
open window.

For a moment, in the strong contrast of the shade with the sunlight
outside, I could see nothing. By degrees it grew more plain. It was their
parlour into which I looked. There was the old open chimney with the
broad oak beam above it. The beams across the ceiling were black with
age. A big bowl of cowslips stood on the table, covered with brown,
shining oil-cloth in the middle of the room; and on a Victorian horse-hair
sofa against the further wall, there lay an old woman, the oldest woman I
think I have ever seen in my life. She must have been near a hundred
years old. Her face was so wrinkled and her skin so shrunken and white
that it seemed, had you pricked her cheek, no blood could possibly have
come. She was asleep. My knocking had not wakened her. I crept back to
the door, lifted the latch, and entered.

She *was* asleep. I crossed over on tip-toe to her side, and for a moment
stood there, listening. Her breathing was like the faint stirring of leaves
in the willow trees by the side of water on a day in summer when
nothing but a willow leaf is fine enough to tell you of the wind. But it
was even and regular. An old clock upon the wall ticked just twice as fast
as came her breathing. I counted it.

It was only for a moment I thought of waking her. It was more I
thought I could not than I could. Then I crept out of the room into the
back part of the house, thinking surely that there I should find the
farmer's wife. Again, no! My search was not fruitless, however, for in
the kitchen there was a cradle standing some few feet from the fire – quite
safe, – and in the cradle there lay asleep a minute little baby. To my
unpractised eye, it might have just been born. For as the old lady in the
parlour seemed to me the oldest person I had ever seen in my life, so this
infant appeared to me the youngest. And these two, sleeping there in
absolute peacefulness, were the sole guardians of the security of Yarningdale Farm. I found no one else – not a soul.

So then I crept out of the kitchen, my heart in my mouth lest I should
waken them, and, continuing my progress of discovery, found at last the
dairy. There, on cool dark slabs of slate, were five large shallow cans, full
of milk. Choosing the one on which the cream had scarcely settled – for
when one is a thief one can still ape the gentleman, – I filled my jug and
crept back again into the parlour. There on the table, beside the bowl of
cowslips, I put some money, and taking a little piece of paper from my
pocket I wrote : 'I have taken a pint of your milk from the dairy without
disturbing either of your babies.'

Only I wrote it in printed letters, because they tell me my writing is
vile.

XXIX

THE COMPLEAT ANGLER

I called him compleat because, had he not been a fisherman, both life for
him and he for life would have been the most pitifully insufficient.

We saw him in the distance as we came towards Preston Bagot, and,
from the strained motionlessness of his attitude, I got it into my head he
was at that crucial moment in a fisherman's day – not when he has a bite,
but when he thinks he has. So I ran down the plank to the tow-line mast
and pulled the rope. Fanny was only too ready to stop. I would not have
disturbed him in that moment for the world.

But it was a false alarm, as I soon found out when I descended to the
tow-path and had come up quietly to his side. This attitude of tensity he
maintained the whole time while I stood and watched him.

'Any luck?' I asked presently, which is the proper and conventional
thing to inquire of your fisherman, showing, as it does, a lively interest,
without casting any slight upon his skill.

He shook his head, but never looked up at me, never taking his eyes
from off that red-and-white float, depending motionless in the water
from the end of his line.

'How long have you been here?'

'Since breakfast.'

'And caught nothing?'

He shook his head again.

'P'raps you've got a bad place?'

'None of it good round here,' said he. But I detected no note of regret
in his voice; he did not say it in the tone of one who yearns for what he
has not.

'Then why not give it up?' said I; 'you're only wasting your time.'

'Nothing else to do,' he replied.

'Why, are you taking a holiday?'

'All holidays now,' said he.

'How's that?'

'Little while back,' he said casually, 'I fell forty feet.'

Fell forty feet! My heavens, but he was proud of it! That casual voice,
that abrupt announcement, were both indicative of his pride. He was like
the pedlar I met outside Wormleighton. He did not wish to tell a lie about

it. He would never have informed me it was thirty-nine feet. That would not have been true. No, it was forty feet, and there he was to tell the story.

'I was laid up six months,' he continued presently – 'twelve operations. I've got a silver plate in my head – two fractures in my right arm, one in my left. One leg's cut off below the knee, and I had three ribs broken. Forty feet's a good tidy distance, you know. You can't fall forty feet without having something to show for it.'

'But do you mean to say,' said I, 'that that's all the damage you received?'

There is a certain sweetness in the pleasure of taking down a man's pride even when he has gone so far as to fall forty feet to arrive at it.

'You fell forty feet!' I continued mercilessly, 'and that's all that happened to you!'

Then he did look round at me and with such as expression of injured dignity as multiplied my simple pleasure a thousand times.

'Ain't that enough?' said he, 'a compound and a simple fracture, an amputation, a silver plate, twelve operations? Why, one of the nurses said to me I was as good as a full hospital to a medical student. Well, I know the biggest I ever heard of a man falling and still being alive was twenty-three feet. I had it sent me – a cutting out of a paper. I fell forty.'

'Did you measure it?' I asked.

'No, but a pal of mine did. It was off of a scaffold. When he saw I was alive, he went and measured it afterwards.'

It was then I saw how, not only had he achieved greatness, but that greatness had been thrust upon him.

'It must have made you a lot of friends,' said I.

He turned back his eyes to his float.

'At any rate, they think more of it than what you seem to,' said he.

'Oh, I think it's a fine performance,' I replied; 'but I must say, if I'd fallen forty feet ——'

'Do you think you'd have more to show for it than what I have?'

'Well, for two days subsequent,' said I, 'I think I should; after that I hope they'd bury me – as decently as the circumstances permitted.'

'Oh, yes – you mean it 'ud have killed you.' he added triumphantly. Then he looked round again and sized me up and down. 'And I expect it would,' said he; 'but you see I got over it. I can come here and fish. I can't work, but I can come here and fish.'

'Well, it's mainly a matter of taste,' said I. 'If ever I fall forty feet – and I think twenty would be quite enough for me, – we shall find that our tastes differ. It's only right that they should. The world would be a damnably uninteresting place if every man who fell forty feet preferred that it should kill him outright rather than leave him with a single capacity for fishing.'

He took his line slowly out of the water, and very thoughtfully – if, indeed, with a silver plate in his head one is capable of any thought – he put more bait on the hook. He had probably had it in the water since mid-day without any at all.

I was about to turn away then and go back to the barge, when a notice-board on the other side of the hedge caught my eye.

'NOTICE – All persons fishing in this water without proper leave will be prosecuted.

£1 REWARD

will be paid to anyone giving information that shall lead to a conviction.

'W. SHAKESPEARE,

'Preston Bagot.'

'Is this gentleman any relation?' I asked.

He looked over his shoulder.

'Of mine?' said he.

'No,' said I, 'of one they used to call William Shakespeare. Is his name William?'

'I don't know,' said he; 'they call him Jim.'

I tried to think of something I might say to that, but the simplicity of it defeated me. W. Shakespeare, and they called him Jim! Perhaps a fond mother had christened him William without any thought of plagiarism, but with the loving hope that one day – you never can tell – he might – But I took it he had not, since now they called him Jim. How merciless and unerring in its judgment the public is!

W. Shakespeare, and they called him Jim!

That is the subtlest form of criticism I have ever heard.

XXX

PRESTON BAGOT

How did they come into existence, these names of the country villages in England? Who had a hand in the making of them? Lowson Ford, Marston Meysey, Princes Risborough, Monks Risborough, Abbots Salford – in all parts, in all counties, you will find such names as bring pictures to your mind, full already of illumination, though never may you have seen the places themselves.

Even Preston Bagot has a sound about it, a sense of aloofness which stamps it once and forever with a joy of the country. But the names of cities – at least to me – mean nothing – Leeds, Birmingham, Manchester; only London has a sound of its own, a throb, a pulse, as of some great thing which is alive and moving. For the rest, there is not the faintest suggestion of choice between them. I would as soon go to Leeds as to Birmingham, as soon to Birmingham as to Manchester. Yet suggest but a visit to Midsummer Norton, and though one may never have heard of the place in one's life, the very sound of it is an invitation.

I felt as sure I should like Preston Bagot as I was certain, when once I had come there, that it fulfilled all my expectations. The canal itself wound in and out, with countless turnings through meadows all in one generous garb of cowslips. Nature seemed never so lavish as this spring. If my compleat angler was a whole hospital to a medical student, then certainly the meadows near Preston Bagot and the woods in the Golden Valley were a whole book on botany to all those who might wish to read.

There are at least three, if not four or five, locks in the short distance between Lowson Ford and Preston Bagot. Their massive arms are the one feature without which the landscape of a canal would be much the same as any other. It is a fine moment, too, when the gates are shut and first the sluices are opened. It is not a matter of interest that I should count the times, but they were many, when I stood at the lock head and watched that first wild rush of water bubbling and bursting upwards like the eruption of a mighty volcano. There follows one moment then, when the surface of the water is prophetically still, as though before another and a greater outburst. But the second is never so mighty an upheaval as the first, and one by one they diminish until there is only that trembling shimmer as when you see the quivering of heated air against strong sunlight.

And slowly and slowly as she lifts in the rising water beneath her, the thick rope fender on the nose of the barge grinds with a gentle purr against the worn lock gates. These are the things you notice on a barge. The life is as quiet as that.

In some of the canals – as on this to Stratford – so quiet is it that I wonder why they keep the lock-houses in existence. The work of the lock, indeed – so much of it as there is – is left mostly to the lock-keeper's wife, while he pursues a more remunerative labour elsewhere. I doubt, in fact, whether these people are any longer in the pay of the canal company. Doubtless they rent the lock-house in the ordinary way of residence, and that is all.

Certainly at Preston Bagot the good woman, with an endeavour to supplement her husband's wages, had placed in that window which looked on to the canal a piece of paper on which was written, 'Here Beer.'

'There's something emphatic about that,' said I, as the water raised us above the lock side and I found it staring at me.

'Look you, sur, that's a clever woman who put that there,' said Eynsham Harry. 'I never felt so close to a glass of beer in my life.'

Whereupon he walked straight up to the lock-house door and knocked and the next minute had put himself in such proximity with it as allowed of no possible comparison. When he came back, he laid his hand upon his stomach and, with a wry smile on his face, said, 'Here beer.'

It was the only jest he attempted to make in all that journey. All other things he said, in which I found cause for laughter, were spoken in the characteristic seriousness of his nature, wherefore I was constrained to laugh at them within me, which is not wholly unenjoyable. A laugh with oneself is better than no laughter at all.

At some short distance from the lock-house the canal winds past the Manor Farm. It must be the finest example of half-timbered house there is

left in England. Leicester's Hospital in Warwick seemed nothing to be compared with it.

'That's where I would live,' said I, 'if I had a dog's chance of it.'

'You've said that, sur, of at least four houses since we be started.'

'I shall go on saying it,' said I, 'as long as I see places like that. There's no harm in a man wishing to live where he can't. He hasn't to pay rent for it. If ever the misfortune befell me to find all the houses empty that I wished to live in, then I might be in a poor way.'

'Well,' said he, "tis a thing I don't understand, living in houses. Why a man should put a roof over his head and make a wasp's nest of it, wi' one room here and another room there, cutting his space up into so many little pieces till there ain't nothing left of it, that's a thing I never shall master. It seems peculious to me.'

Straightway, then, we began an argument which lasted us all the way to Stratford. And upon my soul, I believe I got the worst of it.

XXXI

A CURE FOR TRIPPERS

If I were to write of Stratford-on-Avon, I should be doing myself an irreparable injustice. I have one recollection of the place, but it is not associated with the time I went there on the *Flower of Gloster*. It will remain with me when I have long forgotten the architecture of the Memorial theatre and the Birthplace only clings faintly to my memory. I shall, in fact, always keep this recollection. It is of a lady dressed in white, seated in a pure-white gondola, propelled on the waters of the Avon by a gondolier all clothed in the same colour of virginal simplicity. Whenever I hear of Stratford, I think of that.

We should never have gone into the town this time, only that we needed supplies, for there was a long detour to be made before we came to Tewkesbury, upon which I had set my fancy. I wanted to make my way through Gloucestershire and the Cotswold Hills, and when it came to the next morning I shirked the brunt of that beating back; for we must go over our own tracks almost to Birmingham before we reached the junction of the Worcester Canal. Now I could not bear the thought of Birmingham again, so I sent Eynsham Harry back on the barge with instructions to meet me next day at Evesham.

'I'll join the canal there,' said I, 'and walk along the tow-path towards Tewkesbury till we meet. Have you ever traded on the Evesham Canal before?'

'No, sur, and 'tis my belief there's scarce a boat goes along there now – not unless they be steam.'

'Well, we can't make any mistake,' said I cheerfully. 'It's the river Avon, and I have it here on a map; 'tis navigable. I shall walk straight on from Evesham to Tewkesbury, and we shall meet somewhere on the way.'

We never met for some days, and then not until I reached the wharf at Tewkesbury. But little miscalculations like this will happen in the best of well-planned journeys. I should have missed almost the best part of the adventure had I not buckled my knapsack to my shoulder and set out from Stratford that morning to walk to Evesham.

Now, if I had not done this – which in itself was a treachery to all my scheme of a journey on a barge – what should I not have lost? The fact of the matter is, you must wear out at least one good pair of boots if you are to

know anything about the country in which you live. And once I had started, I could have worn out ten pairs, only that it was arranged that I should join the *Flower of Gloster* on the next day.

Seven miles out of Stratford you come to the little town of Bidford, with its bridge of many angles, which has borne the weight of Warwickshire traffic for four hundred and thirty years. In the days of King John, this same Bidford was the dowry of the Princess Joanne, when she was wed to Llewellyn, Prince of North Wales. Wonderful days were those, when a king could thrust his hand into the purse of his kingdom and draw forth such a dowry as this for his daughter's marriage. I wonder what would be the expression of feeling in Clapham if that idyllic spot were given away as dowry to a foreign prince? You never know – it might become quite fashionable.

Yet, notwithstanding all the romance of its past history, Bidford has but little interest now. In the last twenty years it has been cruelly modernised, due, doubtless, to the fact that it has become the haunt of the Birmingham tripper. I am sure the tripper is a necessary evil. They must find the light of air after days of darkness in these black cities. But between the tripper and the ordinary traveller there is all that difference which exists between the wasp and the bee. The one goes about in swarms, eating and drinking on every possible occasion; the other you will find but singly, heeding nothing but the pursuit of his labour.

I shall never forget the sight of a half-eaten packet of dirty ham sandwiches lying cast away on one of the windows at Versailles. In every village, in every place of beauty or interest, there should be a poisoned public-house to catch the thirsty tripper. He would die as willingly as any wasp in a poisoned bottle; what is more, he would die in a complete sense of gratification, feeding himself until that moment when oblivion came softly to his side, and the packet of half-eaten sandwiches would drop from his lap on to the floor.

If only this were done, there would be no orange peel in Petit Trianon, and Bidford might still have been a dowry fit for any princess.

XXXII

AN OLD NUNNERY

Soon after I had left Bidford I met two old women with white sun-bonnets and sun-browned faces, who directed me on my way to Evesham.

'Turn first turn to the right,' said they in a chorus, 'and keep on away past the nunnery.'

'The nunnery?' said I.

'The nunnery,' said they, and on I went with quickening steps.

At first sight of it, this old nunnery in Abbots Salford almost took my breath away. It was an annihilation of all time. I was back again – if indeed I had ever existed in that period – in the days of Queen Elizabeth. Had a man walked down the grey slabbed path to the lichgate entrance in a silk hat and a tail coat, I should straightway have clapped him into armour or blotted him out of my sight altogether.

It would seem that scarcely a stone has been altered and, except for a small addition which was made to the house some two or three hundred years ago, now well hidden by trees, it must be just the same as it was in the days even long before Elizabeth, when the little nuns kept their farm and fed their poor and saved their money.

The floor within the great high wall is stone – huge slabs of grey toned rich with yellow age, which make you shudder to think of the coldness of the winter nights. I rambled all over it from cellar to roof, paying my sixpence – which is the charge – to the little girl who, thank God, so

unlike a guide, took me from room to room with a whispered 'Would you like to see the priest's hole?' 'Would you like to see the dormitories?'

I liked to see everything, and I think the dormitories, where all those little sisters slept like sparrows close beneath the roof, was the most redolent of the history of the place. It was one colossal chamber, stretching with its massive beams from one gable to another. Here, in one long row, there was accommodation for at least thirty sleepers; for, as I strongly suspect, they had no beds raised from the ground, but slept on straw mattresses ranged along the floor.

At each end of this great room, lighted, not with small dormer windows, but fine, high mullioned spaces that looked wide across the breadth of country and flooded the interior with light, there was a recess where doubtless the sisters slept in charge of all the little nuns.

I cannot help calling them little, for however big she may be in stature, a nun is slight in mind – a child, whose thoughts will never grow into womanhood, who will never know a greater pang than death, which indeed she woos as though he were a lover.

Two hours I spent within the nunnery, peopling each room, for it was a place that gave you a thousand stories without one effort of yours in the creation of them.

Only the chapel disappointed me, for that is still used as the Roman Catholic place of worship in the district, having all the signs of modern Catholicism about it – the cheap finery, the gaudy altar cloth, the ill-painted pictures of the journey of the cross around the walls.

When once I had seen that, then the spell of the place seemed to be broken and I left it, wishing I might have carried my memory of it away

without just that one discordant note.

Yet I suppose it is better to believe than to feel. The few who come there to that little chapel gain a thousand times more comfort from their Mass and Benediction than should I have done in keeping the feeling of the place alive in my memory by its absence.

'The selfishness in this world,' said I, as I walked back to the lichgate entrance, 'the selfishness in this world is abominable.'

Now, I have always noticed that when a man's conscience makes it imperative that he should accuse himself, he does so in the meanest way possible. He generalises. 'The selfishness in this world,' says he. Had he to credit himself with a virtue, he would give the world none of it, and phrase his sentence in a very different way.

XXXIII

FLADBURY MILL

At Evesham begins the so-called navigable part of the Avon. I knew directly I had reached it that I had all the walk to Tewkesbury before me, for Eynsham Harry was quite right – nothing but steam barges could make their way in that water. The tow-path had long been overgrown; only here and there could I discover signs of it.

So I put my best foot foremost and reached Fladbury that evening, where I agreed with myself to stay the night.

There was something about Fladbury Mill and Fladbury Ferry which brought me back to those days when I was a child. Had I spent the first ten years of my life at Fladbury Mill, I should have had a more splendid time even than I had in a house on the edge of a wood, which fulfilled for me then all the great mysterious qualities of a real forest. For in Fladbury Mill and the river running by it, in the broad, tumbling weir, in the secret waters, and the deep, deep lock behind the mill, I could see all the possibilities of a thousand inventions, adventures that would have lasted well through the long summer holidays, and held all their interest and enchantment until the term be sped again.

Instead of Mrs. Wicks, who surreptitiously used to give me of her gloriously home-made toffee from the buttered frying-pan in which she was wont to make it, I can see Mrs. Izod, the ferry-woman at Fladbury, supplying me with radishes from her baskets. This does not please me in contemplation quite so well as the place itself, for radishes would never take the place of home-made toffee – never! But all the rest of it, that was full of tales just waiting to be spun out of the palpitating imagination of some child living at the mill. Maybe they are being told now; maybe they were being told that day when I was there, by the two children, a boy and girl, who were rowing up the river in a leaky old boat – quite possibly those tales were being told then; those adventures were afoot under my very eyes, only I had grown too old to realise them. I am glad, however, that I was not so old as that I could not see their possibilities of them myself.

With just a boat, such as those two children had, how real could Red Indians become in their birch-bark canoes at Fladbury Ferry! What pirates' ships could not be made out of any old thing that floated on the

waters of a river in such a place as that!

For some long time – an hour, it may well have been – I sat down by the ferry-slip and thought of all the splendid things that could be done with only two essential possessions – just childhood and a boat. How easily might that sleepy mill become the frowning Tower of London, to which, by water and the Traitor's Gate, all prisoners were brought for execution! How easily might all the stirring history of England be written through again at Fladbury Mill, with just childhood and a boat!

For childhood, like Nature, can make history with whatsoever comes to hand. It is only when he has reached to man's estate that a child must build castles, set precious stones in crowns, and pave the streets with gold before he can write a year into the book of history.

And Fladbury Mill is such a spot where a pair of children, unbridled and free, could set all history a-humming with their deeds. I wish I had been born at Fladbury Mill! How many thousands of times Mrs. Izod, as, lazily, she pulled the ferry-boat from one bank to another, would not have found herself attacked by a pirate's cutter, boarded, and every passenger thereon made to deliver up their wealth and walk the plank! It would only be pretence, that walking the plank, I have no doubt, but still, a matter easily accomplished while one looked the other way, lest in their pretence the illusion had been spoiled.

This is but a little of all that Fladbury brought to me as I sat by the ferry-slip and watched the water tumbling down the weir. I even caught myself speculating on a race between two flat flecks of foam as, collecting at the bottom of the weir, they started off down the river, neck and neck.

Here, too, the swallows were skimming the water; up and down, up and down, with endless passages, never seeking rest. I could hear Bellwattle in my imagination asking, with wide eyes of wonder, 'Do they *never* sit down?' But it seems as if they never do.

And then – the more mature, perhaps thereby the less complete of all the pleasures I found in Fladbury – I sat on a bank of the river where a crab tree glowed with pink in fullest bloom, and listened to a trio of three nightingales, who sang and sang and sang until it seemed that not a note was left in all the compass of music which they had not touched.

I have often wondered whether the nightingale was really so fine a songster as repute would have him. Sometimes it has seemed that only because he sang when all the rest of the world was silent has his voice won him a spurious reputation. And when I have heard the notes of a blackbird rising above all the other sounds of day, I have seriously been in two ways about it. But that evening at Fladbury, when the sun was dropping fast behind the square tower of Fladbury church in the distance, I was left in no doubt of it. A thrush was singing somewhere. I heard the blackbird's note as well; but they none of them could match my trio.

There were passages in that song which the mere transcribing to the written stave would desecrate for ever. For they sing that music which you would rather never hear again unless by such executants.

It was while I sat there listening that an old woman – sun-bonneted as most of them are – came round the river meadows gathering sticks and dandelions. In her passing from one field to another, she had to climb a stile, but refused all help of mine in surmounting it. First she handed over her sticks, then her apron-full of dandelions, lastly she climbed herself.

'You're very independent,' said I.

''Tis a good thing to be, sur, while 'ee can. If you be round these parts next year, maybe I'll be glad to taking help of 'ee.'

'And what are you doing?' I asked. 'What are the dandelions for?'

'They be for wine, sur. My old man likes his draught of it after the hot days. He says it be as good as any cider, the way I makes it.'

'And how do you make it?'

'Three quarts of blossoms,' said she, 'to a gallon of water, three pounds of sugar, the juice of lemonses and oranges, and when loo-warm mix yeast.'

'When's it ready for drinking?'

'In three months, sur – three months to brew. There be some as drinks it in a week or so, but I keep mine three months, and I have had some as has been in brew a year. 'Twas well called wine, my old man said – he got quite jolly over it one day, he did.'

'And did you scold him for that?' said I.

'Well, I did begin, sur; but he did say such good things about the wine as I'd made, I couldn't find it in me heart. And he made us all laugh, he did, the way he said things. I've never seen him the same like it since.'

'P'raps you don't make the wine so well,' said I.

'Oh, sur, indeed I does my best.'

'Then I expect you wouldn't really be so very sorry if you saw him like that again.'

'Well,' said she, and her head hung very thoughtfully, 'I sometimes wonders perhaps if he did once take a little drop of it too much, I might know 'twas to his liking.'

'It's a difficult matter,' said I, and I hung my head as well, 'but it's always the way in this world;' and here I spoke very sententiously, as though I would add philosphy to ease her difficulties. 'It's hard to know,' said I; 'you want to make it to his liking, and he never tells you what he thinks of it unless he takes a drop too much. Well, we all have problems like this to settle. Life's not so easy as it looks.'

'Indeed, it is not, sur,' said she, and, bobbing me a curtsey, she picked up her sticks and her apron-full of dandelions. I stood and watched her till she hobbled out of sight.

'My God!' said I to myself, 'if the best of us could be no more beset than that!' and I pictured the prayer she would pray that night to help her in her difficulty. Surely the essence of all comedy and tragedy must be in prayer. If only one could hear them all!

By this time my trio had ended their choiring and had left the crab tree. I walked back in an evening silence then through the meadows, and Mrs. Izod ferried across from the village slip to the mill to fetch me.

XXXIV

WOOL-GATHERING

Some years ago, Nafford Mill was burnt to the ground. No, not to the ground, for the four pink-washed walls of it still stand with their sightless windows facing the evening sun like a palace built upon a Venetian canal. All the interior is gutted. The charred beams have been left to rot upon the ground; the great iron wheels and shafts, distorted into wild shapes by the fierce flames that embraced them, are lying there now in a debris of bricks and mortar. Its only roof is the open vault of heaven. Now the heavy mill-wheel is quite still, the water trickles over its slimy plates, for the chains are all rusted and broken and it will never revolve again.

Yet notwithstanding all this devastation, the wide stretch of the Avon here would be incomplete without its mill at Nafford. It stands there at the foot of a steep green slope of grass where on a crest a small thatched farm-house lies down in the shadows of the apple orchard and gazes through its dim latticed windows to the purple heights of Bredon Hill.

I suppose in its days of labour, Nafford Mill lent more to its surroundings than it does now; then I have no doubt the splashing of the water as it turned the old mill-wheel, the gentle whir of the machinery within, and all those peaceful sounds which accompanied the daily grinding of its heavy stones, made such music in the place as, to those who know their Avon well, must now seem desolate in all its silence. But to one who has never seen it otherwise, Nafford Mill could not well be more splendid than it is. I liked its lonely air, its sightless windows, and its silent wheel. The walls, as they stand deep down in the clearest water, might well be made of marble when the sun is shining on them. And all that fulness of apple-blossom which spreads in the orchard around the hill only adds to the almost transparent suggestion that it gives. Indeed, through the higher windows as you look upwards from below, the blue sky glistens, and it seems not like a building of solid brick at all, but an enchanted palace full of the light of air and gleaming sunshine.

From Fladbury I came to Nafford, by way of Eckington Bridge and
Eckington village, and much as I enjoyed the company of Eynsham
Harry, yet they were glorious were those few days when I walked alone
down the banks of Avon.

Of the countless bridges I passed in that journey, I think Eckington is
the most wonderful, the most picturesque of all. It must date back some
considerable number of years before that of Bidford, for even now it is
the only means of transport between Pershore and Tewkesbury with the

exception of one single ferry across the river. For awhile I stood in one of
its niches where the cautious pedestrian may secure himself against the
close passing of the heavy traffic, and there I watched the waters below
me flowing onwards and onwards to the ultimate sea.

There is no place in the world so suitable to reflection as the bridge
which spans a gently flowing stream. For whether it be wool-gathering,
as I strongly suspect was much the case with me, or whether it be a flight
into the highest realms of philosophy, it is equally pleasant, equally the
place above all others. Herr Teufelsdröckh, had he stood upon a bridge
over the Rhine looking down into the flowing waters beneath him
instead of being seated in his garret beneath the stars, would have arrived
at a more far-reaching philosophy even than that of clothes. There is

something in flowing water so constantly and compellingly changing, something which both arrests yet carries on the feeblest of imaginations, that to stand upon a bridge and watch its even, passing ripples must impel the mind to think, and to think, moreover, of things made mysteries by the mutable laws of life. It is coming from whither? It is going whence? And therewith your mind begins its journey from the far-off mountains to the distant sea, until, lost in the limitlessness of a dim horizon, you inevitably return unto yourself, the minute yet living

atom standing upon that bridge in the silent country – you, the smallest speck in this great ocean of space, who, in the flash of an eye, can cast your mind into the distant corners of the earth and yet are there, still standing as I was upon the bridge at Eckington.

It meant nothing – I got no further; yet at moments I had that feeling which Eynsham Harry had so deftly described – I felt that I was on the verge of one of the greatest secrets in the world. It seemed to grow so simple until, from the sheer greatness of its simplicity, it escaped my grasp, and once more I found myself wildly struggling in a seething whirlpool of complexities.

It was no good. I knew that I could arrive at nothing, for I was no more than one particle in all that volume of water which had passed beneath me as I stood upon the bridge of Eckington; I was no more than a drop being carried on and on, just capable of locating myself, of speculating upon my existence while in the narrow river of life, then lost again, perhaps lost forever in the limitless eternity of the sea.

I left the bridge at last. My wool-gathering, or, as no doubt I may have called it, my philosophy, had brought me nowhere. However much it strives, the mind cannot escape the body; however far it travels into space, it must return. In no little feeling of the despair of it all, I walked on then into the village.

At the very entrance of it there stands a Roman cross, around which, on summer evenings, the old people sit and gossip. Sometimes they call them butter-crosses, for here, some two hundred years ago, they came

on butter-market days to sell their wares.

With the exception of its old Norman church, Eckington is just the quiet Worcestershire village, having no particular beauties to recommend it. But in its day, I fancy that Eckington was bigger than this; its close proximity to the bridge must in other days have made it a common resting-place.

Through Eckington, then, I passed on to Nafford, where in the little thatched farm cottage I was given a dish of tea, and set out afterwards to climb to the summit of Bredon Hill.

Half-way up this hill, from the crest of which it would almost seem that the whole of England lay stretched before your eyes, stands Woolas Hall with its fine old tapestries and its minstrel's gallery. I gather this information from the book of a Mr. Charles Showell, who, more fortunate than I, was admitted to see the place, and has drawn in his book of the Avon a picture of the fine old gables of which I could catch but a glimpse while the groom was informing me that only friends of the house were allowed to come within.

This, as I believe I have said before, is quite as it should be. If an Englishman's home really be his castle and his flag is not concealed within the boot-cupboard but flying royally and egotistically from his flag-staff, then the intrusion of a stranger within his gates must be little

less than an abomination. I certainly deserved to be turned away. In these matters a vagabond deserves everything he gets. So really I never saw Woolas Hall; but what with a glimpse over the coachman's shoulder and such imagination as not even an English gentleman can deprive me of, I can picture the glorious place that it is.

Yet better than any mansion was the sight of the country from the summit of Bredon Hill.

'God,' said I, as I stood up there and gazed across the wide stretches of fields so many hundred feet below me, 'God is more generous of his pleasures than is any man.' Which, by the way, is what one only has the right to expect.

XXXV

APPLE BLOSSOM

It was a whole village wrapped in apple bloom. And in the light of that sunset, like snow on the mountains, it was burnished with a glow of pink. You could scarcely see the cottages for all those sheets of blossoms; indeed at a distance, as I walked towards it, only the square tower of the old Norman church rose above this mass of burning white.

This is the village of Little Cumberton in the month of May. It is a colony of apple orchards. They surround every cottage, make the greater acreage of every farm, and almost every garden, it seemed, had one or two trees to bear them fruit.

To add to this, the cottages themselves, half-timbered, are washed white between the beams; the trunks of the apple trees are all painted with lime as well. Never did I see even linen more spotlessly white than was this little village in the shadow of Bredon Hill. If ever Nature can be said, where the presence of man is unavoidable, to look immaculate, it was here. But immaculate is not really a good word. It has so often been used to describe the modern dandy in all his glory of attire, that it has lost the meaning for which alone I use it. Little Cumberton was immaculate, but only to those who know what I really would infer.

I stayed the night there in an old farm-house in the heart of the village. Their garden also had its apple trees; it had its tulips, its forget-me-nots and its Aubrietia beside. The farmer's wife had her eye for colour. But she had planted her tulips in lines so straight that when your eye ran along them as they stood beneath the windows, you could see how uneven were the old walls of the house itself.

The latticed window of my bedroom looked over clouds of apple blossom to the narrow street of the village. I asked that my bed might be moved across the room and placed directly under the window. This was done with all the willingness in the world; and when it came to ten o'clock, I retired, undressed, and lay beneath the clothes beside the open window watching the light of the moon as she drifted through a fleet of clouds which seemed to lie at anchor over Bredon Hill.

There is as much a joy in sleeping close to Nature as there is in being close to her awake. Again and again I closed my eyes, when there would creep into my mind the never-ceasing stir of traffic which echoes through every hour of a London night. And though it was now more than three weeks since I had heard it, the sound of it plainly reached my ears. It was not until I had opened my eyes again to watch the silent traffic of the moon across those dark streets of the sky, that the real stillness of the world came back to me.

The last thing I remember was the soft cry of an owl, and then, perhaps I only imagined it, I thought I saw something heavy and white fly cumbersomely out of the darkness of the trees across the light of the

moon and into the darkness once more. I may only have imagined it, for the next moment I was asleep.

In the morning I woke early. The sun was on my face, a slight breeze was tapping the branch of a climbing rose against the window pane.

I turned on my side and looked out. The village was still asleep. Presently I heard a dog barking – those short, excited yaps as when he is eager about his business. Then there came a flock of sheep, followed by an old shepherd and the dog himself. The shepherd was taking them up to their pasture on the hills. A little cloud of dust from the white road wrapped around them as they walked. Before they reached the end of the street it folded them out of sight. I heard the dog barking now and again in the distance, and before the sound of it had died away, there came the sharp snap of a window catch let loose. I heard the rattle of the latticed panes as they swung back against the wall of the house. It was the village stirring – just awake.

XXXVI

TEWKESBURY

Tewkesbury has not suffered as have Banbury or Bidford. It is as old as the hills, you might say – and without fear of hopelessly being plagiarist, for the hills surround it. So far as I understand, rather than having increased its trade, Tewkesbury has lost it. Some of the old mills are empty now – the wharves are deserted.

There I met Eynsham Harry again, faithfully in charge of the *Flower of Gloster,* waiting with an even and contented mind for me to fulfil my promise and turn up eventually by the canal side. When he saw me approaching, he came forward to meet me with that strange lateral swing of the hands which all bargees have acquired from long walking between the locks. It seems to help them to their pace, for they swing to every step with an automatic action which is inseparable from their stride.

'I told 'ee, sur,' said he first thing, 'that 'twas only steam-boats they'd take down from Evesham.'

'It makes no matter,' said I. 'It isn't because I like boating so much that I'd have anything to say against Shanks's mare. She's an amiable beast, and 'll go mostly anywhere.'

'You rode, then, sur? And here have I been wasting my sympathies on you, thinking how you'd be a-walking. But who might be Mr. Shanks? I've never heard of 'en.'

I explained. I should have thought the phrase might have reached him; but they have queer phrasing of their own. Not that I heard much of it from Eynsham Harry. I often thought that notwithstanding he could neither read nor write, yet he was rather a cut above the rest – perhaps because they could.

'Well,' said I, 'there are three more days before our month is up. I'm going to take a stroll round the town, and then we'll start. I want to go through the Golden Valley and then on to Lechlade.'

'I'll get provisions, sur, and whenever you're ready, that am I.'

So I walked round the old town of Tewkesbury. It is full of strange crevices, and at every turn there looms above the house-tops the splendid tower of its historic abbey. A lot of the work in it, dating from the twelfth century, still remains in wonderful preservation. But thank heavens, I know nothing about these things, and cannot even talk of

architraves and bastions in such a way as would make this chronicle too dull for any but an architect's apprentice.

The sight of it delighted me, none the less. At every corner as it rose above the old Tudor buildings, it reminded me of Rouen. How well, indeed, they have preserved their atmosphere there. It is the town as it was, and Tewkesbury is much the same.

There are passages in the streets there, thrust secretly in between the houses where you would least expect them. Glance down them, and you

might almost believe the sixteenth century were back again. Old half-timbered gables lean across the narrow spaces until they well-nigh touch each other. All this is bound to create a sense of mystery even to the dullest imagination.

I wished then, when once I had seen a little of it, that I had time to see it all. It is so closely written into the pages of England's history that it is a lesson, if it be nothing else. And I for one, at least, have need of such teaching. But having walked down two or three streets and being come but half way down a fourth, I saw a crowd of men and women gathered round some man, to whom they listened while he talked with flowery gestures and that so-called persuasive tone of voice. Now, had the kings of England all been buried at Tewkesbury, I would rather have stopped to listen in this crowd than see a whole row of their tombs.

The man who can hold a crowd is worth listening to, whatever rubbish he may be talking, and it is mostly rubbish that you hear. I stayed once to listen to an orator in Hyde Park.

'Mr. Heggarty will now speak to you on Home Rule,' said a voice,

and thus the new-comer was introduced to his audience. For half an hour
he held them spell-bound. They turned open mouths to him, swallowing
every word. Yet for half an hour that man never finished one sentence,
never made one complete statement in all the words that came between
his lips.

'He's a grand speaker,' a man in the crowd whispered to me in an awed
voice.

'He is indeed,' said I: 'what's he saying?'

'I don't know,' he replied abstractedly – 'he's talking about Home
Rule;' and then his mouth opened once more as he returned the fulness of
his attention.

'I wonder,' said I, as I walked away, 'I wonder if that's the secret of
success in the noble calling of politics?'

But this was no politician in the High Street of Tewkesbury. He was
none the less striving to convince his public of what God knows he could
never have believed himself. He was offering painlessly to extract their
corns with the filthiest instrument I have ever seen in my life.

'Ladies and gentlemen,' he was saying as I came up; and that was wise
of him, they liked that very much. One and all, they felt constrained to
listen when he addressed them so.

'Ladies and gentlemen,' and with his flowery gestures waving his
awful forceps about him he kept back all small children, who crawled in
through people's legs, 'if any one of you is sufferin' the tortures as come
from sweaty feet, let him sit down here openly on this chair as I've got
for the purpose, let him sit down and have his collosities painlessly
removed. I don't mind whether they're hard or soft, white or black, let
him sit down here, and in less than thirty seconds he shall have his
collosity in his hand, roots, fibres, and all.'

Then, as he surveyed the crowd for a likely patient, his comprehensive
glance fixed steadily on me. I felt a sudden consciousness of my feet at
once. They say, if you look at a person's boots it unnerves them. It is
sufficient for a chiropodist to look you in the face. What is more, I am
sure that everyone else in that crowd upon whom his wandering eye
chanced to fall, felt just the same as I. In fact, I saw them gaze down
nervously at their boots, and if the glance continued, they would then
stare at the buildings opposite, as though they were more concerned with
what was happening there. I stared at the buildings opposite myself.

He was a greasy fellow, this journeyman. With his soft black hat, his
long yellow hair, and his black frock-coat, he was much more like a
photographer than the chiropodist he called himself.

'George Schofield is my name,' I heard him saying presently, when I
felt it safe to return the full mead of my attention. 'I'm a professor of
chiropody – a surgeon chiropodist. Now, when I say professor,' he
continued, 'I don't mean a self-titled idiot. You've 'ad some people

coming 'ere to Tewkesbury – I know 'em – I've met 'em. I've stood in the crowd same as you're doing now, and I've 'eard the nonsense they talk. Professors!' His contempt was large, comprehensive. A young farm-hand, meeting his glance, withered visibly beneath it. 'Why, I've seen one of them almost bleed a poor woman to death, the way he hacked at her. Now, that's not my way. With this little instrument in my 'and,' he held out the rusty forceps, that all might see it who chose, 'I'm an artist. I've had my degree at a college. I'm not only known in Stroud

and Gloucester – I'm known all over the country. I've extracted collosities from nearly all the crowned heads of Europe.'

I suppose wearing a crown upon your head has much the same effect as wearing boots upon your feet. It was the first time I had ever heard it, and, in any case, is not a nice thing to think about.

'Well, now,' he went on, 'if anyone has a collosity and wants to be operated on, let him not be ashamed. If he's done no sin let him not be ashamed. Lady or gentleman, there ain't no harm in any of these people seeing your feet. Don't be modest about it. Why, I've got a letter 'ere – there's 'ardly a post but what I don't get one – from a lady I operated on in London.' He began feeling first in one pocket, then in another. 'It was from a lady in 'Ornsey. I took three corns out of 'er one foot. Now, where is that letter? Well, any'ow, she thanked me for what I'd done – thanked me from the bottom of 'er 'eart. That was the way she put it – "from the bottom of my 'eart." "Walking," she said, "is a pleasure. Where before I used to drive in my motor," she said, "now I can walk."'

'Dommed if I'd walk an' I'd a motor,' said some envious fellow in the crowd.

'You wouldn't,' said Schofield; 'but these ladies in London likes a little walk now and then – keeps 'em fit. They don't get no other exercise. Paying an afternoon visit, they like a walk sometimes.'

Especially, thought I, those ladies in Hornsey.

'Well – 'oo's going to take a seat?' persisted the professor. 'You don't mean to tell me that with all the work you 'ave to do, gentlemen, keeping the 'ome going, that you don't 'ave corns! Why, there was a gentleman in Stroud – retired, 'e was – retired – living on 'is own. 'E never 'ad no work to do at all, and 'e 'ad six corns – three on one foot, three on the other. "You sit down, Mr. Capel," I said – that was 'is name – "you sit down, and I'll take 'em out for you in as many seconds." He didn't believe me at first. "I've been suffering with these," said he, "for four years," he said. "You'll only suffer six more seconds," said I. So 'e sat down, and in a whiff they was all lying on the floor by the side of 'em. "Ah," said he, "you've done very well with those corns, Schofield; but I've got something even you can't tackle." "What's that?" said I. "An ingrowing toe-nail," said he. "Sit down there again," said I, "and I'll have it out in two minutes." "What!" said he. "Yes," said I.

'Well, I took it out, and he was proud of it; he was going to put that along with the six corns in his pocket to show to his wife when he got 'ome. But I stopped 'im there. "Oh no," said I, "if you take the toe-nail, I must 'ave the collosities." So I got 'em – we split the difference, and 'ere they are;' and, taking a bottle from a black bag on the ground, he held up those touching remembrances of his art, which, when he shook the bottle, floated nebulously in some dirty liquid before our eyes.

There comes a moment when even an orator of his persuasion loses hold upon his audience. It was at this moment that Mr. Schofield, surgeon chiropodist, lost his hold upon me. I edged my way out of the crowd, and, far down the street I could hear his voice still raised in tireless eloquence. At last there was a lull. I looked back over my shoulder. His soft black hat no longer rose above the crowd surrounding him. I guessed, then, he was operating at last. The artist was at work. I hurried on with a sharp pain suddenly tingling in my feet.

Now, of course, I wish that I had seen more of Tewkesbury instead of listening to the cajoleries of this journeyman chiropodist. Yet in those two short hours before we started upon the last stage of our journey, I saw much to make that time a memory. There is great nobility in it. The ring of battle still lingers in its name. They say Queen Margaret weeps o' nights in Bloody Meadow for her son. If the departed spirits still cherish the sorrows which they knew on earth, then I am sure she must, for Tewkesbury is full of the spirits of the past.

XXXVII

THE GOLDEN VALLEY

When you join the Thames and Severn Canal at Stroud, it is but twenty-eight miles and a few odd furlongs before you come to Inglesham, where the water of the canal joins the Isis and all signs of the tow-path are lost to you for ever. But those twenty-eight miles are worth a thousand for the wealth of their colour alone.

Immediately you have come to Brimscombe Basin and the high land, studded with the grey Gloucestershire houses, begins to rise at either side the canal, it is no longer the English scenery you might expect, but like mountain villages in Switzerland, thousands of feet above the level of the sea. I have seen villages in the heart of the Apennines which reminded me of Chalford and St. Mary's crossing. The mills and the factories with blue slate roofs make a colour against that golden distance, the distance of the Golden Valley, to which, through all those little villages on the hill-sides, you feel you are always leading, slowly and surely, like a miner who knows that the day will come when he shall strike his reef. There is an aura of gold everywhere. The distance is no longer blue – that is more the colour of all the nearer foreground. But away beyond it there is a mist of gold into which all tones and shadows melt like metal cast into a furnace. Mills and factories, blue slate roofs and grey houses! All this sounds impossible; but it is true!

Wherever there is a field in which pasture is left to grow, there the grass is of a golden green, accentuated, there is no doubt, by the sheets of cowslips which are spread everywhere in every open space.

Yet this is but the beginning of the Golden Valley, the long courtyard to that garden through which you must pass before you come to the great gates which give you entrance to this deep valley of gold. And all along by the side of this paved courtyard there grow in broad white feathered masses the flowers of cow-parsnip. At one spot, on a pathway the other side of the canal, there is a door set in a wall that the path itself may continue. Here was the greatest cluster of all. I pointed them out to Eynsham Harry.

'Nature has a wonderful eye for effect,' said I, 'when she sows her flowers. Look through that doorway. Where could you get a better place for a mass of those cow-parsnips?'

His eye followed my hand.

''Tis the fault of most people, sur,' he replied, 'when they plants gardens, to have things in rows, so you can count how many there be. I never had a garden myself – we none of us do, a-boating, – but when I sets some cowslips or blue-bells in a bowl on the cabin, I puts them all in a lump. They looks better that way.'

I remembered then how many a cabin roof I had seen decked with a bowl of wild-flowers. I had seen birds in cages too, carried through their

own fields and meadows, chafing against their captivity. I asked him if he could explain that.

He shook his head.

'Look you, sur,' he said presently. 'There be some persons in this world as have no more sense of the feeling of dumb things than what they'd have of a stone. What's more, they'd think you was daftie if you said them birds weren't made to sing in cages, and had no more taste for it than you and I would have for a week's job on the treadmill.'

''Tis more customary,' said I, 'for them to call you a sentimentalist – though no doubt your people mean much the same when they call you daft. Both accusations are supposed to make you feel ashamed of yourself.'

'Well, sur, if I could open the doors of half the cages I sees on the boats, I wouldn't mind how ashamed I felt. Most like I should get over it, which is more'n the bird 'ud do if he was left in the cage.'

Soon after Chalford, the grey houses with their blue slate roofs grow fewer in number, the hills at each side become higher; there are broader

pasture fields; a stray farm or a lock-house is all you can see of human
habitation. In the nearer distance, the dense woods spread over the
rolling land and, like an army in glittering mail, with golden trappings
and with coloured plumes, they march down the hillsides to the water's
edge.

This part of the country must be the most luxuriant in the whole of
England. In a half-hour's ramble through those woods while Eynsham
Harry was preparing the mid-day meal, I counted seventeen various sorts

of wild-flowers then in bloom. There were bluebells and orchis – those
deep-red purple orchis with their spotted leaves which, in the midst of
the dark violet of the bluebells, made such colours as they wore in the
great days of Rome's Empire. Could the imperial toga have been indeed
as imperial as these?

I found the cuckoo-pint as well, its livid finger in that pale fragile
sheath of green. There were nettles, red and white, but with such bloom
as would shame many a hot-house plant in London. Veronica was there,
with its tiny blossoms that might match the cobalt of any Chinese
dynasty you liked to name. Garlick I found, and primroses hiding from
the heat of May, the last I knew that I should see that year. The violets
grew so thickly, I could scarce but tread them down. Ground ivy
crawled in every open space and, with roots dipping in the cool water,
there were forget-me-nots, king-cups with blossoms of metallic gold and
lesser celandine, apeing the glories of their sovereign.

I found strawberries in blossom and the purple flowers of common
bugle. There was Herb-Robert with its brilliant scented leaf, stitchwort

and salvia. I have no doubt I missed a great many more. There must have been knotted figwort, there must have been white and purple comfrey. I saw no plants of willow herb, yet they must have been there as well. But I had no time to count them all, their abundance was so overwhelming.

And with all these jewelled flowers, imagine a valley of gold. The leaves of the countless trees all set before you in the golden flush of youth; the fields upon the other bank dipped in the gold of a myriad buttercups and cowslips; the sunlight streaming on it all from a cloudless

sky in May – gold – all gold – a priceless valley paved in gold and precious stones.

When I came out from the shadows of those woods into the sunshine again, I could only stand and wonder, wonder what any man would say – his first words – if on a magic carpet I could whip him up from the grey streets and plant him there where I stood. It would probably be something in the nature of blasphemy, but acceptable nevertheless to the God who made it all – far more acceptable as a genuine meed of praise than any prayer of thanksgiving grudgingly offered in a consecrated church.

I returned silently to the barge; as silently sat down to my mid-day meal. Presently I became conscious of the fact that Eynsham Harry was watching me while I eat.

'What is it?' I asked.

'I be waiting for you to taste that dish, sur,' said he.

It was a dish of green vegetable, looking as much like spinach as anything else. I thought it was spinach.

'Where did you get it?' I inquired.

'Would you be so good as to just taste it, sur,' he repeated.

I obeyed, looking up at him as I did so with that pensive expression which I am sure all professional tasters must adopt. You must put on an expression when you specialise. It is part of your uniform, whether it be in the tea factory, the pulpit, or the house of parliament. All specialists are actors.

'Tastes like asparagus,' said I. 'Where did you get it from?'

Still he would not tell me.

'You like it, sur?' he persisted.

I tried another mouthful.

'It's better than asparagus,' said I.

'Put a little pepper wi' it, sur.'

I put a little pepper and tasted again.

'By Jove,' said I, 'it's damned good! Where *did* you get it?'

He pointed to a line of hedge half-way up the hill.

'There be hops growing up on that hedge, sur,' said he; 'these that you're eating be the young shoots, cut off about six inches from the top and boiled the same as other greens. In the month of May we takes 'en whenever we can. The wilder the better.'

'I'll remember that,' said I; and I have, but can find no hedges in London where the wild hop-vine grows. I shall think of it, however, when next May-time comes. I shall surely taste that dish again.

XXXVIII

THE GOLDEN VALLEY – *continued*

For more than three miles the canal divides the wooded hills, a band of silver drawn through this valley of gold. Lock by lock it mounts the gentle incline until it reaches the pound to Sapperton tunnel, and at the summit spreads into a wide basin before it passes into the last lock, some few hundred yards before the tunnel's mouth.

The whole way from Stroud upwards is almost deserted now. We only met one barge in the whole journey. An old lady with capacious barge bonnet was standing humming quietly to herself at the tiller. That was the only boat we found on those waters. The locks are, however, good; some of them have only just been made within the last few years. But the draught of water is bad; in some places we just floated, and no more. It was stern work for Fanny then. There were times when I thought the tow-line must give way, the strain upon it was so great.

In one short pound more shallow than the rest, we came upon two little boys bathing. One was swimming manfully, making great pace and great commotion, struggling as though for dear life; while the other, knee-deep in the shallow water, stood by in undisguised admiration. I strongly suspect the swimmer had one leg upon the bottom. I could always swim so well like that myself. I know too how splendid it looks, for if you make a splash enough there is not a soul can see.

After our meal we went on through the rest of this wonderful valley. It was golden to the last. Even in the water itself the weeds grew more luxuriantly than I have seen in any river. In and out of the forests of trailing weed the fish moved mysteriously, like mermaids in a fairy-tale. It was all a fairy-tale beneath that water. There were dense growths, and then clear spaces on to which the sunshine fell in brilliant patches. The pen of Hans Andersen could have found many a story in that magic country beneath the still water of the canal.

At the top of the valley, looking down between the hills through a lattice-work of apple blossom, stands the Bricklayers Arms, a little inn with two or three houses clustered round it. An old man there described to me the opening of the tunnel in the reign of George IV. He had not seen it himself.

'My big grandfather' – this was how he told it to me – 'my big grandfather, the day the tunnel was opened, he was walking down the tow-path, and he met a feller coming along, and he said to my big grandfather, "Where are you going, my man?" "I'm going to see the king," he says. "I am the king," says the man, and gives him a guinea; and when he looked at the head on the coin, I'm dommed if it worn't.'

It was rather nice, that little touch of human incredulity. I can see him comparing the likeness with that of the head on the coin, catching the face in profile before he finally made up his mind that he was being told

the truth.

The passage through that tunnel of Sapperton, which, on a sudden bend of the canal, opens a deep black mouth into the heart of the hills, was the only time when the voyage of the *Flower of Gloster* had in it the sense of stirring adventure. Into the grim darkness you glide and, within half an hour, are lost in a lightless cavern where the drip drip of the clammy water sounds incessantly in your ears.

Some time ago, when there was more constant traffic on this canal, there were professional leggers to carry you through; for there is no tow-path, and the barge must be propelled by the feet upon the side walls of the tunnel. Now that the barges pass so seldom, this profession has become obsolete. There are no leggers now. For four hours Eynsham Harry and I lay upon our sides on the wings that are fitted to the boat for that purpose, and legged every inch of the two and three-quarter miles. It is no gentle job. Countless were the number of times I looked on ahead to that faint pin-point of light; but by such infinite degrees did it grow larger as we neared the end, that I thought we should never reach it.

'What used the leggers to be paid?' I asked after the first mile, when it seemed all sensation had gone out of my limbs and they were working merely in obedience to the despairing effort of my will.

'Five shillings, sir, for a loaded boat. Two and six for an empty one.'

I groaned.

'A pound wouldn't satisfy me,' said I.

'No, sur, I suspects not. It's always easier to do these things for nothing.'

For an hour that was all we said. For an hour I legged away, thinking how true that casual statement was – 'It's always easier to do these things for nothing.' It is – always. All labour would be play were it not for payment. The man who reckons is worse than lost, he is made; than which there can be no more bitter a punishment. Once, then, the labourer is paid, he begins a-reckoning of his hire, and that is all. From this come revolution and anarchy.

But one does not think of this sort of thing for long while legging it through Sapperton Tunnel. A drip of shiny water on one's face is quite enough to upset the most engrossing contemplation. I saw the pin-point of light growing to the pin's head, and still we laboured on, only resting a few moments to light a fresh piece of candle or take breath.

It was evening when we came out into the light again and, though the sun had set, with shadows falling everywhere, it almost dazzled me. A barge in the next lock rose above the lock's arms, with every line cut out against the pale sky.

XXXIX

HARD-BOILED EGGS

The sense that an adventure is drawing towards its close makes the future look somewhat desolate and uninteresting. After Sapperton and the Golden Valley I felt as if the end had come already, though there were many miles of water to traverse before we reached the last lock at Inglesham.

I was harking back over the last three weeks, the amazing sunlight in it all, the glorious country; sitting, I have no doubt, in an attitude somewhat disconsolate. We were passing under the bridge at Latton, where the road runs over the canal and frames with its arch an orchard where the buttercups throw back the sunshine into the apple trees.

'You be very thoughtsome, sur,' said Eynsham Harry presently, whereby I made certain he had been watching me.

'I'm thinking,' said I, 'that in a few days I shall be back again in London, and the band will be playing Gilbert and Sullivan in Charing

Cross Gardens. There will be a roar of traffic from the Strand, and a dull incessant thunder of the trams along the Embankment. By eight o'clock the whole night will be full of light signs. Lipton's tea, Dewar's whisky, and Californian wines will be blaspheming the sky. Paper-boys will come shouting past my windows of murders I'd far sooner not know about. There may be a piano thumping its notes discordantly against the music of the band. I shall see the people through the windows of the Hotel Cecil feeding themselves, and waiters running here, there, and everywhere with plates. That's what I'm thinking about. It's enough to make you think, when your holiday is over. And talking about feeding, what have we got for lunch?'

Eynsham Harry shook his head.

'There's still a piece of that tongue, sur, and I can do wi' bread and cheese myself.'

But that was not what I wanted at all. I thought of the chandler's shop where I often get my eggs, of the ham-bone which lies on a plate in the window and for ever seems to be in the last stages of boniness. I should soon be eating those eggs for breakfast again, and wanted, for the last time, perhaps, till next summer, to taste an egg with all its country freshness.

'I want some eggs,' said I.

'There's no place, sur,' said he, 'nearer than Marston Meysey where you might get 'en.'

'And how far's that?'

'Well, sur, you come along the canal here two miles and get out there at a bridge. 'Tis then two miles by the road.'

'I'd walk more than that,' said I.

'Then Marston Meysey's your place,' he replied; and to the village of

Marston Meysey, when we had come to the bridge he spoke of, I started off to get my last meal of country eggs.

It is a winding, twisted road to this little village, with high hedges at either side. Most of the way it was more lane than road. At every turning some other lane led out of it, till I had almost lost my way, and began to despair of ever reaching this Marston Meysey where I was to find my country eggs. Two young women driving in a farmer's trap over a narrow bridge that spanned a stream came to my rescue.

'Turn,' said they, 'to the right where 'ee see the barn, then go on for half a mile; but don't turn to the left. Turn to the right again, and follow the lodigraph wires. 'Twill take 'ee straight into the village.'

'Have you just come from there?' I asked.

They nodded their heads, and the flaps of their linen bonnets nodded with them.

'Well, can you,' said I, 'tell me where it's possible to get some new-laid eggs?'

'They be sold at t'bakers. 'Tis on the right of street as 'ee go into the village.'

I found it right enough then, one of those country villages in England 'the world forgetting, by the world forgot.' It must be miles from anywhere; far from the main road, a miniature colony of people contained within themselves.

The baker's was not a shop; just a bake-house, which was a part of an old building standing some twenty odd yards off the village street. In the cobbled yard before it was an old leaden pump, and, with a drip of water falling close to his nose, an old dog lay beneath the spout contentedly asleep until I entered the five-barred gateway into the yard. Immediately he heard the creak of the hinges, he was on his legs and threatening me with a thousand imprecations if I came a step closer.

'Poor old feller,' said I.

He knew that sort of cajoling, and would have none of it.

'You're a cross old fellow, aren't you?' I went on persuasively.

He said that that had nothing to do with it. I had no right in that yard. And I have no doubt the argument would have gone on without my getting a step nearer, had not a girl come out of the house, telling him just what she thought of him and where, if he were worth anything as a dog, he would be lying at that moment. After that he walked sulkily away, muttering under his breath words to the effect that she did not know human nature as well as he did.

'You'd let anybody in,' said he.

'Go and lie down,' said she.

'That's all you can say,' he muttered.

'Go and lie down,' she repeated, and she stamped her foot.

'Don't think much of that for an argument,' he growled, and he tumbled into his barrel, resting his face between his paws, never taking his eyes off me. Even then, he could not keep quite silent, but continued to mumble in a deep note under his breath the word 'Thief.' If you say it in a guttural way yourself, you can just imagine the sound of it.

'He doesn't like strangers,' said the little girl.

'Whereas you trust everybody,' said I.

'It depends what they look like,' she replied.

It was as good as asking me to speak of myself, and as no man refuses such invitation when it is proffered him, I asked her if she meant that she passed me as trustworthy. She eyed me shyly, making me remember that I had not been in the company of her sex for one whole month.

'Well?' said I – and as I said it, I felt my eye meet hers. Now whether there was that in my expression which conveyed my thoughts to her intuition, I would not swear, but she blushed. Then she looked charming, and her eyes dropped. At that moment the dog said 'Thief' again.

'Shall we leave it at that?' said I.

'At what?'

'At what the dog said.'

'I didn't hear him,' said she.

'Perhaps it's as well,' said I. 'Now hadn't I better tell you what I want?'

She nodded her head and, because she thought we were about to begin business, raised her eyes again. Accordingly I talked business steadily – the business about the eggs – for five minutes. The woman who has said she will never speak to you again is always amenable to conversation if you talk business. You may mean what you like – in fact, the more you mean, the more ready is she to talk. Whenever I stopped and she found me watching her, she would say no more. So I asked that the eggs might be boiled then and there.

'I want them for lunch,' said I, 'and have got no place to boil them in.'

'I thought you said you were on a barge,' she replied. 'Haven't you got a stove in the cabin?'

'Thief!' said the dog in the barrel.

'That's quite true,' I answered, and I took no notice of the dog. 'We have a stove and a saucepan and an egg-timer. I told the lie in order to stop a little longer and talk to you.'

Now when you tell a lie to a woman and she knows it is a lie, she is so amazed when you admit it that she takes it as a compliment. A barefaced truth only insults her. What is more, the admission of the lie will often make her laugh. And that is a mood when a woman will forgive you anything.

The little girl took the four brown eggs without a word, put them in a saucepan with some water and placed them on a fire which was already burning in a little niche in the wall. She just added a stick or two, pouring a few drops of paraffin over it to make the whole blaze up.

'I want them hard,' said I.

'You shall have them hard,' said she.

For a while then, we stood together and watched the water boil. Once I looked out of the corner of my eyes to her face to find her staring down into the saucepan, her whole expression full of contemplation.

'A penny,' said I suddenly.

She started.

'One penny,' I repeated.

'Not for twenty pence,' said she.

'Which means,' said I with that intuitive egotism of my sex, 'that you're thinking about me.'

'Do you think a thought about you would be worth twenty pence?' she asked.

'Thief!' said the dog in the barrel.

'Not to speak,' said I, and I ignored the dog again. 'It 'ud be worth more than twenty pence to conceal.'

She bent down and looked into the saucepan.

'It's boiling,' said she.

'So am I,' said I, 'with curiosity.'

'How are you going to take the eggs?' she asked – 'in your pocket!'

'I'll take them,' said I, 'as you give them to me, in my hand.'

'Then I'll put them in a bag.' said she.

And so she did when they were boiled. With her little hand wrinkled already with hard work, she held out the bag by one corner and I took it by the other.

'And now,' said I, 'how much?' but somehow I hated asking it.

'Two pence,' she replied. I don't think she minded in the least. It is only men who are sentimentalists over these matters. They have no head for business when they have a heart to count the coin.

'But two pence!' I exclaimed. 'There were four – four eggs.'

'Halfpenny each,' she replied.

'But the boiling?'

'I won't charge you for that,' said she.

'You can charge me anything you like for the boiling,' said I, stooping to bribery, as is the habit of the best of us – 'you can charge me anything you like if you'll tell me what you were thinking about just now.'

'I won't charge you for the boiling.' said she.

'Fool!' said the dog in the barrel.

XL

DIETETICS

Eynsham Harry had begun his lunch when I returned. A piece of cheese was balanced on a piece of bread, and on its way to his mouth as I came over the bridge.

'I've got four eggs,' said I. 'You must have two.'

'Bread and cheese be all I want, sur,' he replied. And it was all that he ate. It is surprising how little they need, these men whose day is one of strenuous labour from morning till evening. I thought again of the diners and the waiters in London, of the people who consume three and four courses for lunch, six or seven for dinner and a few hours later seat themselves down to supper – not with an appetitie, never with an appetite, but always with the capacity to eat. I thought of the people themselves, men and women who, at the utmost, had done three or four hours' work in the day – the majority of them no work at all – men and women who had never earned a meal in their lives; some of them who had not even made the money to pay for it.

'Oh, you must have an egg,' said I. 'They are already boiled.'

He shook his head.

'Well, how on earth,' I exclaimed, 'do you manage to live on so little? Sometimes you eat an egg for breakfast, bread and cheese for lunch, occasionally a piece of meat for dinner. There are people in London who haven't done half your work, eating meat five times a day and in twenty different ways and dishes. Meat for breakfast, lunch – even meat sandwiches at tea; then dinner and supper.'

'How do they manage to get it down, sur?'

'I'm damned if I know,' said I. 'I suppose much in the same way as you tramp ten miles to find a bird's nest. It's part of their amusement. They could no more walk ten miles than you could eat what they do.'

'Well, sur, then I be glad I be a-boating. I suppose they'd make fun of my bread and cheese. Oh, I be glad I be a-boating. It's good for the stomach. Isn't there anyone to tell them how they be upsetting their insides?'

'There was a play written once,' said I, 'holding them all up to ridicule. They went to see it in hundreds and thousands, but everyone of them thought how well it applied to his next-door neighbour. They knew of everyone whose vice was over-eating – everyone but themselves.'

'Well, that be strange, sur. London's a 'mazing city. They say everything takes place there; but it seems to me that everything takes place outside, and there they only talk about it. Politics be only talk. The country's governed by the people who work. If a new measure's past, it's because men have been working to make the need of it, and they build great houses for folk who can say a lot of words, so that they can talk about what's been done, and not one of 'em knows the way to do it. Do you see this old feller coming along here?'

I looked and, under the bridge, drawing after him a light punt-shaped boat, came an old man with white hair and a soft hat that partially concealed it.

'Who is he?' I asked.

'He keeps the hedges along the canal in order. Trims them up a bit so that the horses can pass by.'

'But no barges do come along here, surely?' said I. 'We haven't seen one all the way from Sapperton.'

'Don't say that to him, sur. He goes on working here day after day all year round, and every night he goes home he expects to find a letter from the Canal Company telling him he ain't wanted no longer. Don't tell him we haven't seen no barges, sur. He'll ask me first thing, and I shall tell him we see one at Kempsford, that place where the canal runs though the village with a high garden wall on one side and apple orchard on the other.'

'That's the last place we came through,' said I. 'I remember it. But tell me, this old fellow gets the pension, doesn't he?'

'He gets it – yes, sur; but he don't spend it.'

'Why not?'

'He prefers working, sur, and this is the last job he'll have.'

He had come up with us by this time, dragging his boat, now nearly filled with the cuttings of the hawthorn hedges, which no doubt he took home for burning.

'Good morning, gentlemen!' said he.

'Good morning!' we replied.

'Have 'ee seen a barge coming down this way from Sapperton?'

'One,' Eynsham Harry replied: 'went back from Kempsford yesterday morning.'

His face brightened, and not only with pleasure, but with recognition.

He remembered Eynsham Harry, and sat down on the side of the barge to talk with him. I looked at his face then. He had the clearest and bluest eye I have ever seen. It might have belonged to a child, yet he was well over seventy.

'Will you have some food with us?' said I.

'No, thank 'ee, sur. I've had my bit a good hour ago.' He pointed to a red and white-spotted handkerchief that lay, wrapped about a bowl, in the bottom of his boat.

'Well, come now,' he continued, taking no more heed of me, but addressing himself directly to Eynsham Harry, ''ee saw a boat. There hasn't been one down these ways, not so far as Inglesham, come the fourth o' last month. I don't know what they be going to do about this canal – there gets less water in her every day, and I keeps at it keeping down the hedges; but you won't see a bit o' horse dung on the tow-path not between here and Inglesham.'

'Well, as long as there's any traffic at all,' I interrupted, 'they won't close it up as long as you're alive.'

'I should be glad to be sure of that, sur. I've written two letters to the people at Gloucester, asking 'em if they thought they wouldn't require my services any longer to let me know, so as I could get work elsewhere; but I gets no answer, only every week my little bit of money. So I don't like to give the job up.'

'No! You stick to it, Willum,' said Eynsham Harry, 'a horse on the path is better'n two in the stable. You stick to it.'

He nodded his head, fully appreciating the advice. We saw him later, when he had gone away, stopping at a hawthorn bush which overhung the path. He was lopping off the protruding branches and throwing them into his boat.

XLI

THE LAST LOCK

The same evening we arrived at Inglesham, where the canal opens wide into a broad basin, across the still water of which the reflections of the high poplars fall with every quivering leaf faithfully traced again.

Along this last pound, between Dudgrove Lock and Inglesham, we passed without saying a word. Most of the time, in fact, Eynsham Harry walked on ahead with Fanny on the tow-path, leaving me to take my last hand at the tiller. It is an occupation to which you get so accustomed that it becomes as mechanical as the mere exercise of walking along the path. Nothing short of complete aberration would lead you to swing the tiller wrong. I have seen a woman steering while at the same time she prepared a meal and nursed a baby. Every now and again she would disappear into the cabin to fetch some dish or other, but never did she steer into the bank or meet the awkward corners beneath some bridge. Steering had become as much a mechanical matter as that with me. I scarcely knew the tiller was in my hands.

At last, as we entered the basin by Inglesham lock, I saw Eynsham Harry lay a hand on the tow-line. Fanny stopped at once, and the rope sagged loose into the water.

'Here's the end of my journey,' said I to myself, and I stepped down into the cabin to get my knapsack, which was already packed. When I came up again, Eynsham Harry was aboard up forard.

'This be Inglesham, sur,' said he.

I nodded my head, and strapped my knapsack to my shoulder. Then we entered into arrangements about his taking the *Flower of Gloster* back to Coventry, where it was to be delivered in good order to Mr. Phipkin, after which we strolled to the lock-head and stood there for a while looking down into the deep basin. Even there the poplars found their reflection. Indeed, they are truly princesses, always standing before some pool to gaze at their own faces.

'Well,' I said at last, 'this is the end of it. Here we part company,' and I held out my hand. He shook it in. a mighty grip.

'If ever you be wanting, sur,' said he, 'to come a-boating again, just write to me at the lock-house at Hillmorton, outside Rugby, and I'll take 'ee out as long a trip as 'ee likes on the *Henrietta*. That's my boat – called after my wife.'

'I'll work my way,' said I, 'if I'm competent.'

'Oh, you be competent, sur, so be you get up early enough of a morning.'

'I shall suit my ways to yours,' said I, 'even when it comes to a matter of birds'-nesting.'

Then he held out his hand, and we shook again, after which I turned on my heel and set off across the meadows for the town of Lechlade. Once I looked back. He had turned the barge round in Inglesham Basin; Fanny was hitched again to the tow-line, and the *Flower of Gloster* was on her homeward journey through those water-roads of England, back to her town of Coventry once more.

COMMENTARY TO THE ILLUSTRATIONS

(nb = narrow-boat)

The 1911 and 1913 editions of *The Flower of Gloster* included W.R. Dakin's line illustrations of scenes mentioned in the text, plus six watercolours – one of the Oxford Canal section, two along the Avon line and no less than three of the final leg of the journey via the Thames & Severn Canal. The 1918 edition was unillustrated. The reprint editions of 1968 and 1972 eliminated the watercolours but supported the line illustrations with some at least of the original series of photographs taken by Temple Thurston. This present edition adopts a different style again.

Thus changes in publishing fashion can be well illustrated from the history of *The Flower of Gloster*. Reviewing the first edition, the Westminster Gazette concluded that '. . . it is a delightful book. The illustrations in colour and black and white, by Mr. W.R. Dakin, are among the sincerest, most spontaneous and charming . . . ever seen in modern books.' In similar vein, the Scotsman's reviewer noted that 'its value is heightened by the excellent sketches by W.R. Dakin in black and white and colours.' Certainly the illustrations formed an important feature of the period 'feel' to the first edition(s).

Similarly L.T.C. Rolt's approach to his photographic selection for the 1968 and 1972 reprint editions reflects the style of the time; . . . 'to be honest' said Rolt, the eliminated watercolours 'are no loss.' The eight photographs relied heavily upon the Stroudwater and Thames & Severn section (five in all) and this selection can perhaps be regarded now as out of balance with the text.

Several factors influenced the selection of illustrative material for the present edition. The best of the original work was to be supported by a much wider selection of contemporary historical photographs, in an attempt to set Temple Thurston's text into something of its original period 'feel'. Assumptions already made about the author's own research on the canal system during the compilation of *The Flower of Gloster* suggested that a broader range of contemporary scenes of canal life – both social and commercial – would further illuminate the text.

In addition, the period of this story – in or around 1911 – lends itself very well to the use of illustrations from the work of contemporary photographers; for this was the period of great activity by town and village photographers recording social life and custom for reproduction as postcards.

Historical photographs speak for themselves. They contribute to our understanding of the social environment of the period in no less a degree than the author's own words. As such, they form a specific contribution to the present edition of *The Flower of Gloster* and are discussed in the following commentary as a study in themselves, rather than being merely – and briefly – captioned under each illustration. The page number for each photograph is shown, and where relevant a reference is given to Dakin's many illustrations in the first edition. The selection is described in a sequence appropriate to the journey undertaken on *The Flower of Gloster*. Colour plates are listed separately.

ii   This illustration aptly sums up many contemporary assumptions of life on the canal system. It appeared for the first time in *The Sphere* on 25th May 1907 with some purple prose making up the caption: '. . . our canals still present a very old world look with their gorgeously painted boats and queer crews for the merry mariners on our canals remain almost the only people who really wear the 'pearly' type of costume formerly associated with the London coster. Whitsun is the season when the bargee appears in all the splendours of new clothes. The picture illustrates the more domestic scenes on board canal boats . . .'. Much of this information is more than a little off the mark. Many working boats looked less than 'gorgeous' for much if not all of their period of use, and the reference to costume confuses one distinctive tradition for another. New clothes must always have been a luxury rarely afforded and certainly not on an annual basis each Whitsun. However the canal community could be characterised by a distinctive dress as later illustrations will show. Note particularly the bonnets of the ladies and the uniformity of the male clothes. For more information, see Avril Lansdell *The Clothes of the Cut*, a history of canal costume (British Waterways Board 1975). (*Photo courtesy Michael Ware, copyright Illustrated London News*)

11   *Surrey* and *Walnut*, two horse-drawn boats from the Fellows Morton and Clayton fleet, one of the best known canal carrying companies. This photograph was published in *The Graphic* in 1910 and typifies the canal scene which left such a marked impression on Temple Thurston. FMC was formed in 1889 from a number of carrying companies on the midland canal system and this scene near Brentford on the Grand Union Canal would have been typical of the traffic between the midlands and London before the first world war. The men seem to be dressed in working clothes whilst the women and children are in their best : blouse and ankle length skirt worn with an apron. Again the bonnets are the most remarkable feature; in black following the switch from white to black at the death of Queen Victoria in 1901 (and maintained incidentally into the 1920's and even 1930's). A stiffened brim across the front and a frill – or 'curtain' – hanging over the shoulders were both sensible precautions against the elements for such an outdoor life. In this respect the young girl on *Surrey* is merely a junior version of the rest of the family – canal children spent most of their lives out of doors. Canal bonnets represented the most elaborate and complicated designs in the tradition of bonnets worn by labouring women of the period. (*Photo courtesy Michael Ware*)

13   Another 1910 view and also on the Grand Union, although this name was not used until 1929 when restructuring took place. Easy to reach from London, this might well have been the canal visited by Temple Thurston and from which he drew some inspiration for his *Flower of Gloster* account. Scenes such as this would not be difficult to find at that time. Here nb *John* and *Joseph*

'breasted up' as a pair of empty boats are worked through lock 55 at Berkhampstead. Both belonged to Joseph Arnold of Linslade and Leighton Buzzard and were used for transporting sand from Bedfordshire to the London area. Only a single horse is being used and this method allowed easier control of empty boats on a wider canal. Note that in contrast to the previous picture, the woman on nb *Joseph* wears a white bonnet. (*Photo courtesy Michael Ware*)

15 Family group with pair of horse boats belonging to Emanuel Smith of Brentford and seen here on the Grand Union. Nearest is nb *Baden Powell* and behind nb (?) *Daventry*. Both on this canal and more particularly on the Oxford Canal at this time, a considerable amount of carrying was in the hands of the owner-operators, the 'Number Ones' whose contribution to canal lore is considerable. Emanuel Smith was one of these, developing a carrying company in his own right. Their story is well summarised by R.J. Wilson in *The Number Ones* (Kettering 1972), the first in a series of booklets on the boating history of the English canal system (the Waterways Museum at Stoke Bruerne stocks the complete series). Little more need be added; this scene suggests something of the serenity of canal life without reference to the long hours, low incomes and poor weather which often accompanied it. (*Photo courtesy Waterways Museum, Stoke Bruerne, ref. BW498*)

17 Another of the 'Number Ones' was Joseph Phipkin who is of course the owner of *The Flower of Gloster* (Chapter VI). Based in Coventry, he would doubtless have worked the canals south to Oxford and London. He is captured by the camera at Buckby Locks on the latter route working a pair of his horse boats back empty to the midland coalfields after a delivery. On the Coventry or northern Oxford Canal, a number of collieries were able to load directly alongside into waiting canal boats. Phipkin's registration reads 'No. 1 G.J. 10940' – the G.J. refers to the Grand Junction Canal before it became the Grand Union, and the boat decoration is typical of its date. Roses and castle motifs show clearly on the cabin doors and the side panel, and the search for the origin of such familiar canal designs has generated a considerable literature. This is well summarised and discussed in A.J. Lewery's book *Narrow Boat Painting* (1974). (*Photo courtesy Waterways Museum, Stoke Bruerne, ref. BW479*)

19 A heavy horse harnessed up for canal work in typical fashion. Note the bobbins along the traces designed to protect the horse against chafing. Bobbins were usually coloured – reds, whites, yellows and blues. The horseman too is interesting – the ubiquitous waistcoat worn undone, with working trousers held up by a large belt and often also by braces. Sturdy boots and a robust hat complete the scene. For a detailed study of canal horses in Britain, see *The Horse on the Cut* by Donald Smith (1982). (*Photo courtesy Waterways Museum, Stoke Bruerne, ref. BW734*)

21 Temple Thurston mentions a steam-powered fly-boat working along the five-mile pound between Marston Doles and Wormleighton on the Oxford Canal (Chapter XXI). Fellows Morton and Clayton were the principal users of steam boats – known as 'engines' to their boatmen – and their last one survived

in use until 1931. Long before then of course steam power had given way to the motor boat leaving this fascinating form of power as little more than an episode between the horse and more modern methods. However it *was* a fascinating period. Here one of FMC's steamers no. 54 PHOENIX (built in 1893 and used until 1925) works through Buckby Locks on the Grand Junction in 1911. 'Fly' working meant (usually) non-stop delivery of perishable or similar cargoes, the steam boats requiring a crew of four to maintain the fast schedules demanded. (*Photo courtesy Waterways Museum, Stoke Bruerne, ref. BW384*)

23   Another FMC steamer, no. 237 MARQUIS approaches the same locks at about the same period, working northwards on the Grand Junction. The space taken up by the engine and boiler (a loss of ten tons of cargo) can be appreciated. This is one of a number of similar scenes recorded on the Grand Junction Canal by T.W. Millner, the resident engineer for its northern district from 1894–1929, whose albums and camera equipment are preserved in the Waterways Museum. His record is indeed a remarkable one – see Michael Ware *A Canalside Camera 1845–1930* (1975). Steamer crews formed something of an elite on the canals; this view shows Captain Sam Slater, mate Dick Lenton and engineer Jim Meese – the first two in typical white cord trousers and the third in 'blue slop'. A visitor enjoys a (no doubt brief) turn at the tiller. (*Photo courtesy Waterways Museum, Stoke Bruerne, ref. BW366*)

25   Another of Millner's photographs showing a further scene at Buckby Locks during a stoppage of traffic in June 1907. Buckby was a 'gauging' lock where boat cargoes were calculated and tolls paid to the canal company. Millner's studies show that it was also a common place for a hold up of this kind to enable essential canal repairs to be undertaken. Whitsun was a favourite period and as many as 80–100 boats might be caught up in this way. Meanwhile life goes on in the cabins of the three horse boats on the right; the larger steamer on the left is another from the FMC fleet. In his own journey Temple Thurston seems to have been completely unaware of such activities on the busier canal routes. (*Photo courtesy Waterways Museum, Stoke Bruerne, ref. BW568*)

29   Another stoppage at Buckby six years later gives us this scene on board one of the carrier Faulkner of Leighton Buzzard's horse boats. A christening has brought out all the traditional dress of the women – full, long skirts, boots and the elaborate black bonnets. The older lady on the left also wears a shawl. Corduroy trousers, waistcoat and flat cap completed the man's dress for the occasion, making good use of the enforced stoppage in an otherwise almost constantly moving way of life. (*Photo courtesy Waterways Museum, Stoke Bruerne, ref. BW380 and BW365*)

31   The family group of Edward Powell at Braunston Top Lock just before the first world war. Whilst the lock is being prepared, the children line up for the photographer – surely one of the most informative and natural groups from the whole archive of canal children's pictures? Tradition and function mix in the clothes, and the two younger children remain on board nbs *Forget Me Not* and *Water Lily*. (*Photo courtesy Waterways Museum, Stoke Bruerne, ref. BW415*).

33 Leaving Oxford at the start of his journey Temple Thurston found the city suburbs depressing (Chapter XI) before he reached the open country. He would have passed canal-side wharves such as this at Hayfield Wharf, from which Frank Restall operated a coal business in Oxford. The date is about 1890; empty boats – swept clean after their delivery – prepare for the return journey to the midland collieries. This site was formerly the earlier terminus of the Oxford Canal later extended into the city to wharves at Worcester Street and New Road. Nuffield College now occupies this site and Hayfield Wharf has also been built over. (*Photo courtesy Michael Ware*)

35 There were nearly 250 bridges over the Oxford Canal to Coventry and on the southern section an interesting group of wooden drawbridges where the platform of the bridge is counterbalanced by projecting fixed twin beams. This bridge was no.241, photographed in 1868 at Walton Well, and little more than an accommodation link between fields on either side of the canal. The roughly hewn tree trunks forming the beams are noteable – so too is the rural scenery of this view, now built over by the Oxford suburbs. (*Photo courtesy Michael Ware*)

37 Banbury interested Temple Thurston (Chapter XV) although he found the
38 town disappointing, not least the famous Banbury Cross erected in 1859 to commemorate the marriage of Victoria, Princess Royal to the Crown Prince of Prussia. It remained, however, something of a focal point in a town which had otherwise lost much of its 'old aspect'. In Parson's Street he found the Reindeer Inn retaining some of its beauties; this 16th century building had its frontage remodelled in the 18th century.
Banbury was once an important canal town and L.T.C. Rolt also had the opportunity to comment upon it whilst tied up there on his nb *Cressy* journeys – see *Narrow Boat* (1944). I wonder what either author would make of Banbury now? (*Photos from Valentines Series postcards, David Viner collection*)

39 The 'glaring modernity of agricultural instruments' caught Temple Thurston's eye in Banbury, where the firm of Samuelson & Co produced a range of implements – and particularly reapers – from their Britannia works throughout much of the Victorian period. This photograph by the celebrated Oxford photographer H. W. Taunt shows a sail reaper at work in an Oxfordshire field about 1900. (*Photo courtesy Cotswold Countryside Collection, Northleach, copyright Oxfordshire County Libraries*)

41 Cropredy on the southern Oxford Canal, and inspiration for no less than four chapters of *The Flower of Gloster* (XVI–XIX). Without doubt Temple Thurston knew this place and this whole section of the journey rings very true. Still a popular canal-side haunt today, Cropredy is relatively little changed. (*Photo from postcard by Percy Simms, Chipping Norton; David Viner collection*)

43 One of Temple Thurston's own photographs captioned 'opening the lock at Cropredy Bridge'. This scene inspired the sketch on page 88 of the first edition of *The Flower of Gloster* and led Rolt to wonder whether the figure on the left was the lock-keeper and – more particularly – whether it was Eynsham Harry opposite him on the right-hand side. It might well have been and remains the

nearest clue from the album of photographs with which Temple Thurston recorded his journey. Notice the tow-rope leading back from the horse to the boat waiting to enter the lock. (*Photo courtesy Mrs E. Temple Thurston and Michael Ware*)

44 A few minutes later with the boat now in Cropredy Lock; the (?)lock-keeper is about to close the gates assisted by a boy who looks as if he too belongs to the canals. A scene which inspired page 67 of the first edition. Mop and watercan sit on top of the cabin in their usual places. Lock, bridge and cottage can still be found at this spot – the bridge being a typical brick structure of the Oxford Canal. (*Photo courtesy Mrs E. Temple Thurston and Michael Ware*)

53 Canal scene at Napton in about 1909 where the Oxford Canal drops down through a flight of locks before skirting round Napton Hill to its junction with the Warwick and Napton Canal, now part of the Grand Union route into Birmingham. This view reveals the relatively open and isolated countryside through which the upper sections of the southern Oxford Canal ran. Temple Thurston has very little to say about Napton, omitting any mention of the distinctive windmill on the hill-top which has been such a landmark for so many canal users in this area. (*Photo courtesy Michael Ware*)

55 Another of the wooden drawbridges which were such a characteristic feature of the southern Oxford Canal, and usually isolated as here amongst the fields. (*Photo courtesy Michael Ware*)

57 Temple Thurston's album contained several photographs believed to have
59 been taken of working scenes along the Oxford Canal. Two of these might well be linked to one pair of boats owned by Joseph Coles. In the first nb *Lilian Rose* has the tow-rope pulled tight from the mast, whilst in the second Mrs Coles steers the butty-boat (the second of a pair) whilst keeping an eye on her baby sitting on the cabin roof. Apart from the photographer's clutter, both watercan and mop can be seen. Mrs Coles wears a striped blouse with a plain apron and a belt – the latter a favourite with both men and women. An informal scene and a useful insight into the responsibilities of the wife in a canal family such as this.
Was the Coles' pair of boats one of the rides which we might imagine Temple Thurston 'hitching' on the Oxford Canal? (*Photo courtesy Mrs E. Temple Thurston and Michael Ware*)

61 A third Temple Thurston picture illustrates nb *Leslie* owned by boat builders Lees & Atkins of Polesworth on the Coventry Canal. This firm was one of a small number used by the owner-boatmen for repairs to their boats, which would often also include re-painting. Without his boat, the 'Number One' would of course also be without his source of income, and so Lees & Atkins and others had change boats available for hire during repair periods. Nb *Leslie* was one such, seen here in the care of a young girl sporting the black bonnet familiar from previous photographs. (*Photo courtesy Mrs E. Temple Thurston and Michael Ware*)

64 Temple Thurston determined to write 'not a word of the history of Warwick' but doubtless had a good look around the town. He listened in to an account of the history of Leycester's Hospital in the High Street. As it now survives, this is a fortuitous group of buildings incorporating more than the original hospital founded by the Earl of Leicester in 1571 in buildings which actually date back to the 14th century. In the 16th century timber-framed cottages alongside were incorporated to give a pleasing terrace effect, offset superbly by the West Gate Chapel beyond. (*Photo from postcard, David Viner collection*)

65 St. Mary's Church was originally a substantial Norman building but was almost completely rebuilt following the extensive fire in Warwick in 1694. It dominates Church Street and much of the town and surrounding area. (*Photo from postcard, David Viner collection*)

67 'A call from the miller'; a timeless country scene captured almost with affection by the photographer about 1890 in Warwickshire. Flora Thompson's *Lark Rise to Candleford* (1945) creates similar images in prose for this same part of the midland countryside. (*Photo Warwickshire Photographic Survey, reproduced by permission of the Local Studies Librarian, Birmingham Public Libraries*)

68 Another view from the Temple Thurston album, captioned 'leaving Turner's Green near Rowington on the way to Birmingham'. This is the section of the journey in which the author grew increasingly unhappy with the environment in which he found himself; the heading for chapter XXV suggests a gloomy mind. No other information is available about this scene, but the boat is being pulled to the towpath side whilst the horse takes the opportunity to graze the bank. (*Photo courtesy Mrs E. Temple Thurston and Michael Ware*)

69 Knowle locks, 'up which we climbed wearily', ended the ten-mile pound with a flight of six locks each comparatively deep and hard to work. In the modernisation programme of the 1930's this flight was reduced to five locks, the previous layout being preserved in part alongside. The next eleven miles which would have taken *The Flower of Gloster* into the heart of Birmingham proved too much for Temple Thurston's sensibilities and somewhere beyond Solihull Eynsham Harry turned Fanny and the boat round and they returned to the open countryside. The scene in this photograph remains a mystery – activity on the towpath seems to suggest a dispute of some kind; date *c.* 1905. (*Photo courtesy Michael Ware*)

70 Warwickshire rural scene at Barston in April 1890. The women wear working dress suggesting a country version of the canal boatwomen's clothes. Exposed brick and timber-work reveal the construction of the cottage. (*Photo reproduced by permission of Local Studies Librarian, Birmingham Public Libraries*)

71 At Kingswood Junction near Lapworth *The Flower of Gloster* left the Warwick line and joined the southern Stratford Canal for a 13-mile journey 'right out of the track of the world'. This photograph shows the flight of locks descending to the junction – always a busy canal centre during the working life of the Stratford Canal and again today. (*Photo courtesy Michael Ware*)

72   Going in the other direction from Kingswood Junction the northern Stratford
      offered then (and still does) a far more scenically interesting route into
      Birmingham than Temple Thurston's intended route. At Drawbridge Road,
      Shirley in about 1923 nb *Blue Lias* belonging to Kaye & Co. Ltd. of Southam
      Works passes under a raised drawbridge reminiscent of the examples already
      noted on the Oxford Canal. The boat is probably carrying a load of cement.
      The building alongside the canal was a cider house. (*Photo courtesy Michael
      Ware*)

The canal link to Stratford on Avon (and hence into the river Avon) was not
completed until 1816 and the canal was of doubtful commercial viability throughout
its working life. Today it is perhaps better known for the considerable volunteer
efforts which lay behind its restoration to through navigation in 1964. In the care of
the National Trust, it is busier today than Temple Thurston would have found it in
1910.

73   One of its more intriguing features is the series of barrel-vaulted lock cottages
      unique to a section of the southern Stratford built in 1812–3. Temple Thurston
      obviously admired them and photographed the almost unaltered (until
      recently, that is) example at the lock at Lowsonford. It was used to illustrate
      page 138 of the first edition. The cottage design may simply be due to
      economy, although it is tempting to accept the story that the barrel roof
      reflects the abilities of the builders who were more familiar with canal
      tunnelling than house-building. (*Photo courtesy Mrs E. Temple Thurston and
      Michael Ware*)

76   Temple Thurston's encounter with the recently-bereaved man on the bridge at
      Lowsonford lock impressed him deeply. The illustration (page 143 of the first
      edition) is called to mind in this photograph of another pensioner in
      contemplative mood, albeit in a different county. The dress is similar :
      working jacket and corduroy trousers plus a trilby worn indoors for the
      photograph. Gaiters indicate an outdoor life, probably of farm work. (*Photo
      courtesy Cotswold Countryside Collection, Northleach, copyright Gloucestershire
      Records Office*)

79   Reminiscent of Yarningdale Farm (Chapter XXVIII), this was the kitchen at
      Ram Hall, Berkswell, Warwickshire in July 1892. There had been no
      preliminary tidying-up, almost as if the photographer had stolen up unawares
      as did Temple Thurston to Yarningdale Farm a few miles away. Farmer
      Thomas Fletcher was obviously elsewhere. The kettle hangs over the fire and
      the kitchen doubles as a laundry, witness the mangle on the right. (*Photo
      Warwickshire Photographic Survey, reproduced by permission of the Local Studies
      Librarian, Birmingham Public Libraries*)

81   Delightful rural scene on the canal system about 1900. Although not photo-
      graphed on the route followed by *The Flower of Gloster*, it typifies the canal
      scenery through which Temple Thurston and Eynsham Harry travelled from
      Oxford to Stratford on Avon. Farm produce is being loaded directly to boats

on the Buckingham arm of the Grand Junction near Maids Moreton, some ten miles in length and last used for commercial traffic about 1938. (*Photo courtesy Waterways Museum, Stoke Bruerne, ref. BW650*)

87   The High Street in Stratford on Avon in the summer of 1890. Both Town Hall and Guild Hall can be seen in the distance. An important market town for its area, Stratford had a good corn market in the Victorian period and the usual range of activities of a country town of its size. Temple Thurston gave it short shrift, along with Banbury, Warwick and Evesham. (*Photo reproduced by permission of Local Studies Librarian, Birmingham Public Libraries*)

89   Another view of women at work, this time in domestic service at a house in Sheep Steet, Stratford, in 1899. (*Photo reproduced by permission of Local Studies Librarian, Birmingham Public Libraries*)

90   Village characters at Bidford on Avon in 1899 – full of local information and reminiscence. Clothes and men look equally worn by a lifetime of toil. (*Photo Sir Benjamin Stone Collection, Birmingham Public Libraries*)

92   The 'Old Nunnery' of Chapter XXXII was at Abbot's Salford in Warwick-
93   shire and visited by Temple Thurston on his walking journey along the banks of the Avon from Stratford to Tewkesbury. Salford Hall is a large stone house in the Elizabethan style, boasting a porch dated 1602 and a gatehouse with a timber-framed gable guarding the entrance. This latter inspired the sketch on page 172 of the first edition. (*Photos from postcards by Walker of Stratford on Avon; David Viner collection*)

95   At Fladbury another of the author's memorable encounters took place – with Mrs Izod, the ferrywoman of the Fladbury ferry. An aged and rather hunched figure working the rope ferry gently across the river Avon, Mrs Izod wears a large white bonnet and working apron (see sketch on page 178 of first edition). The lady clearly left her mark and so too did Fladbury; the combination of ferry, river and mill conjured up a childhood fantasy for Temple Thurston. (*Photo courtesy of Mrs E. Temple Thurston*)

The following seven photographic studies are the work of William Ward Dowty (1887–1979) who learned his craft in his father's chemist and photographer's business in the High Street, Pershore. The studies belong to the period before 1913 when Dowty purchased a photographic business of his own in Worcester which he ran until his retirement in 1959. Much of the excellent work of such local photographers was planned for postcard production, and where archives of negatives survive they can contribute a great deal to a social history of the area during this period. Dowty's contribution to the life of Pershore also included teaching at Sunday school, singing in the abbey choir and serving with the town's fire brigade.

96   This study of Cropthorne or Fladbury mill recalls the sketch on page 175 of the first edition of *The Flower of Gloster*. It is a scene of rustic calm – fishing and sailing model boats on the river – and an excellent example of a postcard

study. The date is *c.* 1910. The Lower Avon between Evesham and Tewkesbury proved a barrier to Eynsham Harry's plan to rejoin the author somewhere along the river, and it seems that he did not navigate *The Flower of Gloster* up-river from Tewkesbury. Only in recent years has the Lower Avon Navigation Trust been able to restore and maintain navigation throughout this 28-mile length – the first restoration project to be completed by volunteers and without the use of public funds. (*Photo courtesy Michael Dowty, Stoulton, Worcester*)

97 Broadway House in Broadway Lane, Fladbury *c.* 1910. (*Photo courtesy Michael Dowty, Stoulton, Worcester*)

100 Nafford mill in the parish of Birlingham, Worcestershire, taken before the disastrous fire of 17th May 1909 which left the building burnt out. This is how Temple Thurston found it (Chapter XXXIV), its brickwork fire-stained and its equipment distorted and abandoned within. An amusing story attaches to the attendance by the Pershore Fire Brigade on this occasion; W.W. Dowty was himself a member of the crew and was fined 2/6d for taking photographs of the aftermath of the fire whilst still on duty! Note across the river the sluices which made navigation so difficult. (*Photo courtesy Michael Dowty, Stoulton, Worcester*)

101 The narrow 16th-century stone bridge across the river Avon at Eckington has always been an attractive subject for photographers; this is Dowty's view about 1910. Temple Thurson regarded this bridge as 'the most wonderful, the most picturesque of all' on his journey, and the opportunity for another bout of philosophising. (*Photo courtesy Michael Dowty, Stoulton, Worcester*)

102 Village cross in the centre of Eckington from a photograph taken about 1920. The cross was restored in celebration of Queen Victoria's 1897 Diamond Jubilee. See the illustration to page 189 of the first edition. (*Photo courtesy Michael Dowty, Stoulton, Worcester*)

103 The village blacksmith at work in Eckington in the years before the first world war. The wide and open street and lack of traffic add to the charm of this village scene. (*Photo courtesy Michael Dowty, Stoulton, Worcester*)

105 'It was a whole village wrapped in apple bloom' – this was Little Comberton in May and certainly a delightful place to stay en route for Tewkesbury. This village scene shows well the mixture of timber and brick cottages with thatched and slate roofs. The cottages on the left were frequently subjects for the camera, epitomising 'village character'. (*Photo courtesy Michael Dowty, Stoulton, Worcester*)

The Flower of Gloster omits any mention of that section of the journey which must have been necessary to complete the route from Tewkesbury (Chapter XXXVI) to Stroud (Chapter XXXVII) i.e. down the river Severn into Gloucester Docks, along the Gloucester & Berkeley Canal and into the Stroudwater Canal at Saul. At Stroud this canal made an end-on junction with the Thames & Severn Canal. See the introduction for discussion as to whether Temple Thurston actually undertook this journey in a single circuit at all.

107 However, Gloucester Docks should not be omitted from the contemporary photographic record. This view taken *c.* 1910 shows the fine ranges of brick-built warehouses fronting the main dock. These date from the period 1826–73 and reflect the growth in the corn trade at this time. Gloucester was used by a variety of vessels ranging from coastal steamers to the distinctive craft of the river Severn including the trow. The smaller narrow boat of the canals was also much in evidence. One of the warehouses is clearly marked 'The Severn & Canal Carrying Co. Ltd.' This was the major carrier linking the midland canal system with the Severn and the coastal trade. The name dates from about 1891 although the company had previously existed under a different format and continued to make an important contribution to the life of Gloucester Docks right through to the nationalisation of the waterways.

Here the steam coaster *Stock Force* of Whitehaven is being unloaded into the trows *Avon* and *Wye* as well as directly into Biddles warehouse. For a new study of the city docks, see Hugh Conway-Jones *Gloucester Docks : an illustrated history* (Alan Sutton Publishing, Gloucester, 1984). (*Photo courtesy Michael Ware*).

109 Splendid study of a group of narrow boats in Gloucester Docks in the 1890's. The distinctive decoration is clearly visible on each, providing a contrast in colour to the rather drab surroundings and murky waters of the docks. From the left nb *Perseverance* owned by John Wheeler of Gloucester and with a registration number on the BCN – the Birmingham Canal Navigation system in the heart of the midlands. Second left is nb *Sabrina* (also with a BCN number) and belonging to the Salt Union Ltd., Stoke Prior Salt Works, Worcester – alongside the Worcester & Birmingham Canal. Next is nb *Mary* owned by William Fox of Nuneaton; the fourth boat is tied up bow-first and cannot be identified. All four are laden down in the water and loaded with salt; the Victoria Dock shown here was also known as the Salt Basin. (*Photo courtesy Michael Ware*)

112 Temple Thurston's album contains this interesting view of Stonehouse Basin on the Stroudwater Canal. I wonder whether this was the only working boat he saw during his visit to this area – hence the photograph? The wharf here acquired the name Penn's Wharf after a Mr. Penn who leased it for domestic coal brought down from Staffordshire by narrow boats, and steam coal brought across the Severn from the Forest of Dean coalfield in Severn trows. One such is shown here. The sidings linked with the Midland Railway branch line to Stroud and Nailsworth. (*Photo courtesy Mrs E. Temple Thurston and Michael Ware*)

The remaining eleven photographs were taken on the Thames & Severn Canal which links these two great rivers of southern Britain by a 30-mile route crossing the Cotswold scarp by a tunnel at Sapperton. This canal has been derelict for over fifty years, and represents that part of *The Flower of Gloster's* journey which cannot today be re-created by water. The remainder of Temple Thurston's journey *can* be followed, at least as far as Saul at the junction of the Gloucester & Berkeley and Stroudwater Canals.

The author obviously found his experience of the Thames & Severn as interesting as any other part of the journey, no doubt due in part to its colourful scenery but perhaps also the result of the dereliction and sad decline which must have been apparent in 1910–1. Small wonder then that it is rather better represented in his photographic record than any other part of his trip. This led L.T.C. Rolt to make use of these photographs (with very little prompting, I suspect, for he too had a fondness for the T & S) and such sentiments re-appear again in the present commentary! In truth, this group of photographs tells us a great deal about the state of the Thames & Severn at this very late stage in its working life. For reference, see Humphrey Household's study *The Thames & Severn Canal* (1983 new edition) and Michael Handford and David Viner's *Stroudwater and Thames & Severn Canals Towpath Guide* (1984).

113   At Bowbridge, one mile east of Stroud, a five-man maintenance crew is at work dredging the canal bed just above the lock. Surprisingly this interesting activity merits no mention by Temple Thurston. The process was indeed a laborious one, using a spoon or scoop dredge (formed of a leather bag on an iron ring at the end of a long pole) which was lowered over the side of the dredger, dragged along the bottom and raised by a windlass. The boat is tied up to a convenient mile-post recording the distances from each end of the canal. (*Photo courtesy Mrs E. Temple Thurston and Michael Ware*)

114   Now much changed, but when this postcard view was taken a typical canal scene along the valley of the river Frome between Stroud, Brimscombe and Chalford. At Brimscombe Bridge, the canal approached the inland dock facilities at Brimscombe Port. Today, both canal and bridge have vanished at this point although the Ship Inn survives. (*Photo courtesy S.J. Gardiner, France Lynch, Glos*)

It was just beyond Brimscombe Port, near the bridge and lock at Bourne, that Temple Thurston discovered the spread of cow-parsnip (cow-parsley) which so attracted him, and the arched doorway across the towpath which features in the sketch on page 211 of the first edition. He photographed both subjects for his album.

115   This photograph was also used as the basis for a sketch (page 213 of first edition). It shows Chalford wharf, four miles from Stroud, with two narrow boats tied up on the opposite bank. Today, these buildings have been cleared away for road improvements; the wharf area survives but only as an amenity space alongside a short stretch of watered canal. (*Photo courtesy Mrs E. Temple Thurston and Michael Ware*)

117   The summit of the Thames & Severn was reached at Daneway, after a considerable climb through 28 locks up the valley from Stroud. The hamlet here actually developed around the canal and owes its existence to it; for five years during the construction period (1785–9) Daneway was the eastern terminus for traffic on the canal and a busy place as a result. The Bricklayers Arms (now Daneway Inn) was built at this time, and provided a further

opportunity for Eynsham Harry to enjoy a drink. This view, taken perhaps a decade before his visit, shows wharf cottage, basin and inn (on the left). (*Photo courtesy S.J. Gardiner, France Lynch, Glos*)

118   Temple Thurston's own view across the top lock to the Bricklayer's Arms at Daneway. The lock is now the pub car park. (*Photo courtesy Mrs E. Temple Thurston and Michael Ware*)

119   Another pair of views, one of which was taken by Temple Thurston during his visit. Less than a mile from Daneway is the western entrance to Sapperton tunnel, which runs for two and a quarter miles under the Cotswolds. Each portal enjoyed some architectural embellishment (not enjoyed by all canal tunnels, incidentally) – the western end in a gothic style and presenting a rather overpowering approach for the boatman. This impression was not lost on Temple Thurston! Alongside the tunnel entrance stood a maintenance man's cottage, seen here in this postcard view *c.* 1904 by local photographer W. Dennis Moss. (*Photo courtesy David Viner collection*)

120   By 1911 the tunnel cottage had been whitewashed and here some examination seems to be going on into the state of the canal at this point. Some of the banking of trees which overhang the tunnel entrance has been removed from this picture. A stylised version of the tunnel entrance appears on page 222 of the first edition. (*Photo courtesy Mrs E. Temple Thurston and Michael Ware*)

121   Pleasure boating on the summit level of the Thames & Severn; this is actually on the arm which connected Cirencester with the main line of the canal at Siddington. This picture is contemporary with *The Flower of Gloster's* journey. (*Photo courtesy Corinium Museum, Cirencester*)

122   Another form of pleasure boating on the canal system – three men in canoes work down through the flight of three locks at South Cerney on the eastern section of the T & S as it falls to the river Thames. Date is *c.* 1875–85 and the photographer believed to be H.W. Taunt of Oxford. (*Photo courtesy Oxfordshire County Libraries*)

123   Coming over the hump-backed canal bridge in their trap, these two country ladies dressed in their white bonnets provided inspiration for both sketch and comment in *The Flower of Gloster* (see page 227 of the first edition). The horse wears ear protectors to keep off the flies. Possibly photographed at the wharf at Cricklade. (*Photo courtesy Mrs E. Temple Thurston and S.J. Gardiner*)

128   Chapter XL introduces the reader to another canal figure – 'Old Willum', described by Temple Thurston in his notes as the 'old man with the blue eyes who keeps the canal in order between Latton and Lechlade'. He probably lived in the lock cottage at Eysey (derelict now) and seems in this view – one of three taken here by Temple Thurston – to be coming under the bridge at Eysey Farm. Note that this is built largely of rubble stone, in comparison to the neater brick bridges we have noticed elsewhere. In age and dress this old man compares well with the subject on page 76. (*Photo courtesy Mrs E. Temple Thurston and Michael Ware*)

Sepia reproductions are taken from:

between pp. 26–27: detail of the christening scene at Buckby locks (p. 29); the western or Daneway entrance to Sapperton tunnel on the Thames & Severn Canal (p. 119); and a detail of Joseph Phipkin owner of *The Flower of Gloster* at Buckby locks (p. 17). Between pp. 58–59: detail of the crews from a pair of Fellows Morton & Clayton boats at Watford on the Grand Union Canal (courtesy Waterways Museum, Stoke Bruerne, ref. MN1857); the Edward Powell family group at Braunston (p. 31); and a detail from the High Street view in Stratford on Avon (p. 87). Between pp. 74–75: detail outside Broadway House at Fladbury *c.* 1910 (p. 97); the group of narrow boats in Gloucester docks (p. 109); and a detail from the stoppage of canal traffic at Buckby in 1907 (p. 25). Between pp. 106–107: a further detail from p. 25; Daneway wharf, inn and basin at the summit level of the Thames & Severn Canal in 1904 from a photograph by H.W. Taunt (courtesy Oxfordshire County Libraries); and a detail from another Taunt photograph at South Cerney locks (p. 122).

FURTHER READING

Apart from the titles already mentioned, there is a mass of canal literature for further reference. The Waterways Museum at Stoke Bruerne in Northamptonshire stocks a good selection and so too do a number of other waterway museums and bookshops. See particularly:

The Canal Age (1968) Charles Hadfield *British Canals* (7th edition 1984)
and other works by this author including a series of regional studies of the canals of Britain.
Anthony Burton and Derek Pratt *Canal* (1976)
Harry Hanson *The Canal Boatmen 1760–1914* (1975) and *Canal People* (1978)
Tom Chaplin *The Narrow Boat Book* (1978)
and four studies by Michael Ware making excellent use of historical photographs:
A Canalside Camera 1845–1930 (1975); *Britain's Lost Waterways: vol. one – inland navigations* (1979); and *vol. two – navigations to the sea* (1979); *Narrow Boats at Work* (1980)
P.A.L. Vine *Pleasure Boating in the Victorian Era* (1983) is a useful and recent survey.

ACKNOWLEDGEMENTS

Alan Sutton greeted with enthusiasm the suggestion that a new edition of *The Flower of Gloster* be added to the growing waterways list of Alan Sutton Publishing Ltd., and has encouraged my efforts throughout the relatively short period of time available for its preparation. Others too have been more than helpful with advice, offers of assistance and opinions on the fascinating background to *The Flower of Gloster*.

I quickly found support for my own view that this account was the distillation of accumulated canal experiences. Edwin Cuss of Cirencester and David Boakes of the Stroudwater, Thames & Severn Canal Trust had both used the photographic evidence to advance this view. Humphrey Household once again gave me the fruits of his many years' study of canal matters, generally agreed with my sentiments but felt (as did others) than the portrait of Eynsham Harry was certainly strong enough to have been drawn from life, as indeed we suspect he was. Charles Hadfield contributed in equal measure and in the same vein – support, indeed! – and put me in touch with Mark Baldwin whose *Canal Books* – a guide to the literature of the waterways (1984) – was published during the preparation of this edition. Temple Thurston's volume, he notes, 'is without question a highlight of canal literature'.

Hugh Potter kindly sent me a copy of an article from the December 1972 issue of *Waterways World* (The 'Flower of Gloster' – fact or myth?), the result of which was a most interesting and enjoyable discussion with its author, David Blagrove, in his cottage (excellent bed and breakfast, too!) beside the Grand Union Canal at Stoke Bruerne. Most if not all of our collective thoughts from this article and subsequent discussion have been incorporated in the introduction to this edition.

Sources of the photographs have been noted within the commentary, and are not repeated here. However, special thanks are due to Michael Ware for so readily making available excellent material from his extensive collection of canal photographs, and to Mrs Emily Temple Thurston for allowing access for copying from her husband's photo album some years ago. Edwin Cuss and Stan Gardiner were grateful for this opportunity and a number of prints have been used from both these sources. The excellent collections held at the Waterways Museum will be known to many enthusiasts (and will soon, it is hoped, be known to a wider audience), and the Curator/Manager Tony Conder went out of his way on a busy summer's day to provide facilities for study.

Hereford & Worcester Record Office in Worcester kindly gave me access to its photographic archives, which led me to Michael Dowty and the work of his family's photographic business; the quality of the subjects chosen here is but a small reflection of the value of this collection. At the Bingham Library in Cirencester, Alan Welsford provided study facilities and also conjured up from elsewhere the obituary notices which gave me the framework for my study of Temple Thurston's life and writings.

Finally my wife Linda accepted the intrusion of this latest project with her usual equanimity and give it both support and active encouragement. Her word processor also proved invaluable! My thanks, as ever, to her.

Comments, corrections and further contributions towards the commentary to the photographs would be welcomed, as indeed would knowledge of other contemporary photographs relevant to the journey of *The Flower of Gloster*.

David Viner
Cirencester

The introduction, picture research and compilation of the commentary to the illustrations has been undertaken by David Viner, Curator of Museums for Cotswold District Council. He is a Fellow of the Society of Antiquaries and of the Museums Association, and has an established reputation as an archaeologist and local historian, with responsibilities including the Corinium Museum at Cirencester and the Cotswold Countryside Collection, a new and developing museum of rural life at Northleach.

He has published a number of volumes of historical photographs of this area, including *Cirencester As It Was* (1976), *Old Cotswold Photographs* (1977), *Transport in the Cotswolds* (1981) and *Victorian & Edwardian Cotswolds* (1983).

He is also a canal enthusiast, particularly for the Thames & Severn Canal, and author of *The Thames & Severn Canal* (1975) and jointly with Michael Handford the more recent survey *Stroudwater and Thames & Severn Canals Towpath Guide* (Alan Sutton Publishing 1984). A number of other papers and articles discuss the history of this Cotswold canal.
